The Organizational Storytelling Workbook

This workbook is an interactive guide for leaders and managers to help you tell compelling stories at work. *The Organizational Storytelling Workbook* offers:

(a) a critical engagement with academic debates on organizational storytelling; and

(b) a series of exercises designed to allow users to improve their capability as organizational storytellers.

The text begins with a chapter which locates organizational storytelling within a critical account of organizational cultures. This book argues that managerial accounts of organizational culture offer a limited appreciation of the ways in which people think, feel and act, and suggests storytelling as a means of redeeming our understanding of all matters cultural. Having secured this new appreciation of culture and storytelling the workbook develops a series of maxims and exercises designed to allow users: (a) to improve their storytelling practice; and (b) to reassess the cultural assumptions and priorities revealed through their practice.

Enriched with interactive features to walk managers practically through the process of improving their storytelling skills, including practical exercises, contemplative questions and space to respond creatively to the ideas in the book, this workbook is the perfect companion to any executive or postgraduate course in storytelling as well as a useful and enjoyable companion to any individual manager that wishes to improve their skills.

David Collins is Professor in Management at University of Northumbria, Newcastle and the founder and Managing Director of Gain Insight Ltd, a consulting organization offering bespoke services on HRM, organizational change/transformation and the application of narratives to organizational problems. An academic with more than 30 years' experience, David holds advanced degrees from the universities of Glasgow, Strathclyde and Essex. This is his sixth book. Previous works published by Taylor & Francis, Routledge include *Organizational Change: Sociological Perspectives* (1998); *Management Fads and Buzzwords: Critical-Practical Perspectives* (2000); *Narrating the Management Guru: In Search of Tom Peters* (2007); *Stories for Management Success: The Power of Talk in Organizations* (2018); and *Management Gurus: A Research Overview* (2021).

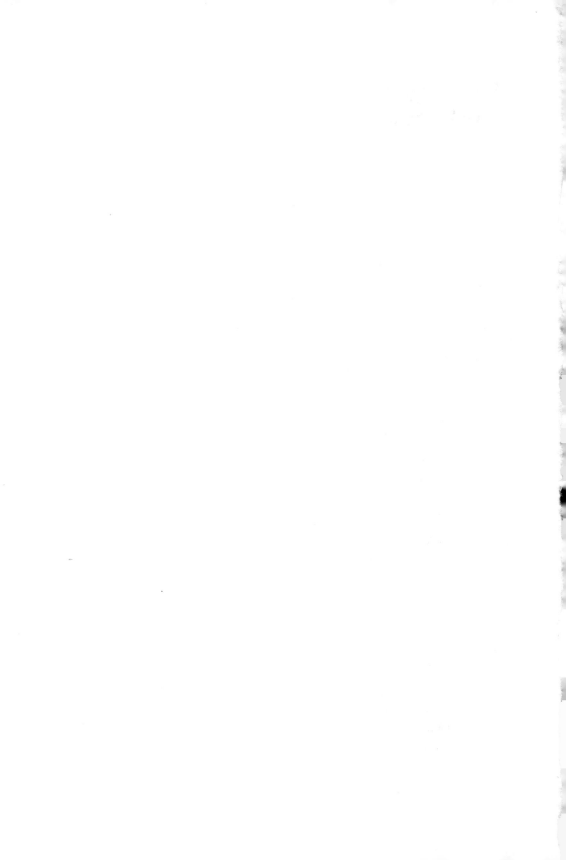

The Organizational Storytelling Workbook

How to Harness this Powerful Communication and Management Tool

David Collins

Routledge
Taylor & Francis Group

LONDON AND NEW YORK

First published 2021
by Routledge
2 Park Square, Milton Park, Abingdon, Oxon OX14 4RN

and by Routledge
52 Vanderbilt Avenue, New York, NY 10017

Routledge is an imprint of the Taylor & Francis Group, an informa business

British Library Cataloguing-in-Publication Data
A catalogue record for this book is available from the British Library

Library of Congress Cataloging-in-Publication Data
A catalog record has been requested for this book

ISBN: 978-0-367-90123-3 (hbk)
ISBN: 978-1-003-02275-6 (ebk)

Typeset in Bembo
by Taylor & Francis Books

Made in Kilmarnock

Contents

Introduction

This workbook has been designed as a companion to *Stories for Management Success: Putting Stories to Work* (Collins, 2018). If you're not familiar with this book, don't worry, I'll talk about its contents and approach in just a moment. Indeed, to those who are late to the party, to those who have just arrived, I offer the reassurance that the workbook you now hold in your hands has been designed to work on its own terms.

I'm not suggesting, of course, that you shouldn't buy *Stories for Management Success*. Actually I believe that you should: It's a good book; I had fun writing it and I really do think you'll enjoy it!

What I am saying is this: The workbook you now cradle comfortably in your hands (and I'll come back to this in a moment) will help you in your organizational life (and everything in life is organizational!) even if you haven't read my earlier book; even if you have never before considered managerial work as an activity rooted in, and dependent upon, the practice of storytelling.

* * * *

If you are already familiar with my *Stories for Management Success*, indeed if you bought my book, I have two things to say to you. First, thank you!

And, second, please don't think that the book you now hold in your hands simply repeats what I have written before. It does not!

This workbook has, of course, been designed as a companion to my earlier work. Yet it is complementary: The opening discussion, which frames the activities of the workbook (developed in Chapter 1), and the maxims developed in Chapter 2 are, for example, genuinely new and, while these chapters will, necessarily, cover some of the ground traversed in *Stories for Management Success*, this offers new content that has been developed specifically for this workbook. Thus the account of organizational storytelling offered here, unlike that developed in *Stories for Management Success*, will frame our core concerns within a critical appreciation of 'culture'. This discussion, as we shall see, (a) challenges much of what has been written for managers on the nature of 'culture' and on the mechanics of 'culture change' while (b) utilising a critical, sensemaking, account of storytelling to redeem this endeavour.

This workbook will, therefore, offer insights on the manner in which sensemaking processes might be interrupted through storytelling in order to enable you (purposefully and deliberately) to have an impact upon the manner in which people think, see and act within your organization.

But before we get to all this … I promised those late to the party that I would make some introductions …

* * * *

Stories for Management Success offers a critical analysis of the key academic debates concerned with organizational storytelling. The book is framed within a discussion of the nature of management and is designed to explore the core and limiting feature of managerial work.

Stories for Management Success observes that the actions of managers are generally framed within an account of 'control' and 'direction'. Yet the painful truth is that managerial control is self-limiting. Indeed it might be more appropriate to suggest that managerial control is limited and self-defeating because organizations – even those that micro-manage; even those that seek to control the activities of their employees on a moment-to-moment basis – depend upon the continuing exercise of discretion and goodwill to secure organizational ends; to develop value for consumers.

This understanding of the self-limiting nature of control is of crucial importance. It reminds us that attempts to secure managerial/organizational ends through the pursuit of direct control strategies will, at best, dampen the enthusiasm of your colleagues and will, at worst, simply extinguish the goodwill that delights customers.

Recognizing the uncomfortable facts of managerial work, *Stories for Management Success* argues that organizational storytelling offers a powerful tool for change. Stories, as we shall see, possess and harness this potential energy of social organization. Storytelling, in short, represents the primary means by which managers may usefully place their visions, their plans, in the company of others who can bring these to fruition.

Yet while advancing the understanding that storytelling is, in fact, central to managerial work, *Stories for Management Success* also argues that much of what has been written on this subject is flawed analytically and is, furthermore, counterproductive at a practical level. These problems persist, I suggest, because managerially oriented accounts fail to locate storytelling within a suitably critical appreciation of the nature of management. Addressing this concern, *Stories for Management Success* reveals and explores the many different ways in which managerial attempts to control the thoughts and actions of others may be undone by more local 'sensemaking' processes.

Building upon this nuanced appreciation of the limits inherent in the practice of organizational storytelling, *Stories for Management Success* concludes with a set of six questions/analytical observations designed to prepare the (managerial) storyteller for the challenges that await anyone with the temerity to announce a tale in an organized context.

Stories for Management Success, of course, does not claim to offer a template for success in storytelling. It is, however, clear that a failure to reflect, and to act upon, the core issues identified within the text will undermine the articulation of managerial goals and, more broadly, support for those organizational orientations preferred by managers.

* * * *

The text which you now hold *ever so comfortably in your hands* (and, yes, I am getting to that) takes up the challenges identified by *Stories for Management Success*. This workbook has been designed, therefore, to allow you to meet and to overcome the challenges associated with purposeful storytelling in an organized context. To allow you to address these challenges this (work)book has chosen a radical design.

* * * *

This book is quite unlike anything I have ever written before. It is a 'workbook'; it is, as we shall see, a tool. It has been designed, for example, with lots of 'white space' which would not have been at all welcome in my earlier works. Indeed you will find that I have placed my text *recto* and have left the *verso* pages for you to inscribe.

In this regard the workbook is, in a sense, incomplete and will over time come to represent a co-production. That said, my name is on the front. That's just how these things work!

The (nearly) blank pages have been placed in the text and placed next to mine because I want you to write in, and on, this workbook. The blank pages therefore have been left blank *for you*. Many of the pages within this workbook are (nearly) blank, therefore, to allow you to make notes; to draft stories; and to doodle (if that's your thing) as you document your reflections on management, culture and on the practices (and pitfalls) of organizational storytelling.

It may also be useful to note that the book has been 'sized' to be big enough to enable you to work on and within the text without (as it were) cramping your style. Yet the book has been designed to be small enough to make it, properly, portable.

This is a text (figuratively and literally) that has been designed to travel with you. It should pass from hand, to pocket, to bag and back again. It should be with you in meetings; on the train; and in the departure lounge.

Friends and colleagues tell me that my library is remarkable because almost all of my books are in 'as new' condition. And this is probably true: I cherish the books I own. Although I should add that I suspect that my colleagues really think that I buy texts (as the English *nouveau riche* did when they acquired their country estates), by the yard and for the purpose of decoration.

I don't really mind how you manage your library. Break the spine. Fold the pages. Annotate the text if you must! But I will say this: I want you to treat this book as *a workbook*. In time it should show signs of age; signs of use. Indeed this book should wear the evidence of its ageing proudly and as a sign of your managerial wisdom.

So … close down the spreadsheet. Fold down the laptop. Those tasks can wait.

Storytelling is your new, number one job. Storytelling is (although you may not realize it yet) your present and your future because managerial success accrues to those who can place themselves, their goals, their plans, their visions and their stratagems usefully in the company of others.

* * * *

This workbook has been conceived to help you, the user:

- To develop a critical appreciation of the nature of organizational culture.
- To enable you to understand the self-limiting nature of managerial work.
- To secure a critical understanding of the nature of organizational storytelling.
- To embed storytelling within an account of organizational culture that explores the limits of this cultural metaphor.
- To improve your ability to craft, develop and write tales which project organizational goals *while* recognizing local concerns and/or anxieties.
- To improve your ability to perform stories within your workplace and within the workplaces of your customers and clients.
- To undertake and to present an audit of prevalent storytelling practices within your employing organization or within a client organization.

* * * *

This workbook is arranged in four chapters.

Chapter 1 offers a lucid yet critical outline of stories and storytelling within workplace contexts. This chapter builds directly upon my earlier work (Collins, 2018) but rather than simply reproduce the gist of *Stories for Management Success*, Chapter 1 will offer an account of storytelling that is rooted within a critical reading of those 'popular management' texts which advance notions of culture change.

This chapter will demonstrate that accounts of culture and its management too often misrepresent the nature of social organization and in so doing block opportunities for cultural change. This failure arises because the avowedly 'practical' treatments of the business of management proffered by 'popular management' adopt a worldview which is unthinkingly top-down in orientation. This worldview, as we shall see, fails to grasp the plural nature of organizations, and thus fails to appreciate that others cannot be assumed to share your preferred reading of the world and its problems.

Chapter 1 will also demonstrate that managerial appreciation of organizational cultures tends to be based upon an overly formal treatment of organizational processes and dynamics. This sanitized account of organizational life, when combined with a top-down orientation, tends either to obscure or to deny the living, breathing people present within your working life and, consequently, the social interactions that construct our organizations … and which you will need to manage!

Offering storytelling as a means to reconnect with these (less formal and more profane) organizational processes, Chapter 1 will:

- Offer a critical reappraisal of 'organizational culture' especially as this is represented within 'popular management' texts.
- Examine the self-limiting nature of management.
- Embed the 'narrative turn' in management within an account of the nature of managerial work.
- Place storytelling within a critical appreciation of culture and change.
- Contrast sensemaking and sensegiving perspectives on storytelling.
- Place poetic storytelling within an account of other, related, narrative forms.
- Consider story-types – the epic, comic and tragic narratives which shape our worlds.
- Offer an analysis of commonly voiced stories which, as we shall see, suggest a disconnection between those stories *transferred* from the top of the organization and those *shared* towards the bottom.
- Pause regularly to invite reflection; to allow users to assess understanding.
- Offer large quantities of blank space to allow additional note-taking and doodling (if that's your thing).

* * * *

Chapter 2 will offer guidance on the challenges associated with crafting and telling tales within organizational settings.

This chapter builds upon Chapter 1, while drawing upon experience gained working with executives in the UK and across Europe. Offering concrete guidance on the practice of storytelling this chapter will re-visit the six questions/pieces of advice articulated in the concluding sections of *Stories for Management Success* and will offer 14 'maxims' for storytelling (we Scots are superstitious) which reflect upon (for example) the need to identify 'hosts'; the benefits of 'meanders'; and the need to play the 'white notes and black notes'.

In addition, Chapter 2 will offer practical tips designed to enhance authenticity in your storytelling practice.

Drawing upon examples from my own biography, from academic research and from the works of novelists and journalists, this chapter has been designed to offer the insights necessary to allow you, the user of this workbook, to understand the practices, processes and potential pitfalls of storytelling at work.

Chapter 2, in short, has been designed to allow you to understand, concretely, the opportunities and the constraints that will shape your tales of life and organization.

* * * *

Chapter 3 will offer a variety of exercises and writing challenges designed to allow you to put the first two chapters of the workbook into practice.

This chapter, made up of more than 20 storytelling exercises, has been designed as an invitation to craft stories. Indeed it has been designed to encourage you to write stories so that these might be developed and refined for future/further application. As you will see, this chapter has been designed to encourage you craft stories that:

- Offer 'epic', 'comic' and 'tragic' tales of working.
- Render your 'first', 'best' and 'worst' days at work.
- Recall a 'screw-up'.
- Recount a situation when you, perhaps against the odds, 'turned things around'.
- Offer accounts of 'lucking out' and 'getting away with it'.
- Reflect upon 'wellness' and 'work–life balance'.
- Consider the challenge of 'digital'.
- Render life from the 'bottom-up'.
- Address the anxieties which arise and persist within contexts where adults, candidly, are allowed to tell other grown-ups what to do; what not to do; when to arrive; when to leave; and, in some settings, *if* they can visit the toilet.

The exercises developed for you in Chapter 3 have been designed to dove-tail with the reflections on culture developed in Chapter 1. In this regard the exercises that you will be invited to undertake offer an opportunity to broaden your appreciation of the storyworld which your organization crafts and (deliberately or otherwise) maintains.

Finally, Chapter 3 will conclude by inviting you to develop (explicitly) what I will call 'more complex tales'; tales which combine, for example, epic and comic story-forms.

These 'more complex tales' are, as we shall see, more sympathetic to the rhythms, processes and travails of everyday life insofar as they mix story-types in order to develop accounts of organizational life that are, I suggest, more appealing. Indeed I would argue that these tales (despite increased complexity) are more likely to be portable in an organized context because they offer a more faithful appreciation of organized life *as it is lived*.

* * * *

Chapter 4 will build upon your co-author's (see, for example, Collins, 2007; 2008; 2012; 2013) analyses of storytelling practices and has been designed to allow you to (re)consider priorities; prevalent themes; and patterns of presence/absence within the context of organized storyworlds.

The exercises developed in this chapter may be used in at least a couple of different ways.

They may be used, first, by those who despite being embedded within a particular context find themselves in a position when/where they need to understand their organization with 'fresh eyes'. I suggest, for example, that those recently promoted to a managerial, or indeed to an executive, level may wish to use the exercises developed here to:

a   develop a new appreciation of the organization and its culture;
b   highlight a need for change; and
c   craft an agenda framed around stories that will secure this aspiration.

Equally, the exercises developed in Chapter 4 may be used by those who have, either, recently been appointed to a new organization (and now need to develop a useful appreciation of its manners, mores and priorities) or by consultants who, because they spend their professional lives moving through the employment concerns managed by others, would benefit from a methodology designed to reveal, quickly and efficiently, the nature of their client's cultures – warts and all![1]

Whatever your need and whatever your agenda, Chapter 4 will invite you to collect; to harvest tales of organization. Having developed a catalogue of tales you will be offered exercises, which (amongst other challenges) invite you to reflect upon the story-types, themes, patterns and, crucially, absences apparent within the storyworld researched. These activities will be used to invite further reflection and, from this, the development of alternative themes and frames designed to facilitate the realization of a (substitute) storyworld that supports individual orientations and organizational goals.

Note

1   This is, of course, a reference to a command said to have been issued by the Englishman Oliver Cromwell who in the 1600s was appointed 'Lord Protector of the Commonwealth of England, Scotland and Ireland'. The artist Sir Peter Ley was duly commissioned to produce a portrait of Cromwell. When asked how his likeness should be rendered, Cromwell is said to have demanded realism such that he should be painted with all his imperfections, 'warts and all'.

References

Collins, D. (2007) *Narrating the Management Guru: In Search of Tom Peters*, Taylor & Francis: Abingdon, Oxon and New York.

Collins, D. (2008) 'Has Tom Peters Lost the Plot? A Timely Review of a Celebrated Management Guru', *Journal of Organizational Change Management*, 21(3): 315–334.

Collins, D. (2012) 'Women Roar: The "Women's Thing" in Tom Peters' Storywork', *Organization*, 19(4): 405–424.

Collins, D. (2013) 'In Search of Popular Management: Sensemaking, Sensegiving and Storytelling in the Excellence Project', *Culture and Organization*, 19(1): 42–61.

Collins, D. (2018) *Stories for Management Success: Putting Stories to Work*, Taylor & Francis: Abingdon, Oxon and New York.

1   Organizational culture; organized storytelling

Introduction

In this chapter I will develop an account of organizational storytelling that is rooted within an appreciation of (a) culture and (b) the nature of management. I have chosen this approach for two reasons.

First, this approach contrasts and yet complements the account developed in *Stories for Management Success*. It will, therefore, advance the analysis I have developed elsewhere rather than simply repeating this.

Second, this means of structuring the analysis will allow us to understand the potential of stories in an organized context while rescuing 'culture' from the clutches of 'popular management'.

We begin with reflections on what is sometimes termed 'the cultural turn' in management studies (Collins, 2000).

* * * *

It is now commonplace to speak of organizations in cultural terms. Indeed whenever a large issue, or seemingly intractable problem, arises, managers, academics, business analysts, police officers, politicians and sometimes even football players (see Collins, 2000) are wont to announce that the matter at hand is, at root, 'cultural' and will consequently require (perhaps) a ten-year programme of transformation.

Following this sort of announcement two things tend to happen:

First, management consultants begin to flick through catalogues, which sell yachts and private jet planes.[1]

Second, the managers, politicians, policy-makers and police officers (I could go on) who have witnessed this cultural revelation all nod, sagely, in agreement.

Yet such superficial agreement as to the need for 'cultural change' and, indeed, the utility of those mechanisms invoked to secure change in the thoughts and actions that constitute our organizations tend to cloak the presence of persistent debates concerning (a) the nature and origins of culture and (b) the processes of cultural reproduction that mark and sustain our organized lives.

Indeed the fact that all concerned tend to agree that the big organizational issues we now face are cultural, at root, signals only that you may secure agreement among wise and foolish alike just so long as you trouble the conscience of neither.

In this chapter I aim to challenge this false consensus on 'culture' so that, together, we might come to understand the complex realities that intrude whenever we seek to intervene in the lives of others. Yet while our interest, here, is critical, conceptual and challenging of taken-for-granted assumptions, our focus remains practical insofar as it is designed to reveal and to explore the contests that shape our organizations and the dilemmas that characterize managerial action.

Do I have sure-fire remedies to offer you? Of course I do not.

And, if you are honest you know that such recipes as are currently available – *How to build great teams; How to deliver useful change; How to manage culture* – simply do not deliver upon their promises.

Noam Chomsky (2003) has a number of rather neat tools designed to test rhetorical statements such as those that commonly circulate in political discourse. Chomsky advises that whenever we encounter a broad, rhetorical claim – '*this is all about freedom*'; '*Brexit is the will of the people*' – we should make an effort to relocate the claim in a separate, parallel, context. If the rhetorical projection fails in the new setting, this failure may be taken as an indication that the claim is, in the context of its original articulation, empty and/or reflective of interests that are narrowly partisan.

Following Chomsky's advice we may now ask ourselves: how would claims made in relation to effective strategies for 'change management' and/or 'cultural transformation' function in an extra-organizational context?

You might like to ask yourselves, therefore, would you spend your own money on a book that promised untold riches, risk-free?

Would you use your own money to purchase tickets for a seminar which promised to reveal the sure-fire secrets of a happy family life?

Would you purchase a book that promised to teach you sure-fire tactics for dating success?

If your answer to questions such as these is, 'No, of course not', then please read on.

If your answer is, 'Yes please share your sure-fire, success secrets with me!', then I have a catalogue of wares that may be of interest. Please log on to: www.please_take_all_my_cash.com so that you and your money may be parted.

I am joking of course. I don't (presently) own this domain-name. But my humour, however weakly expressed, has a serious intent, for I want you to understand:

a   that so much of what practitioners (whether they be managers, politicians or footballers) think they know of 'culture' and 'cultural change' is limited, distorted and skewed in ways that seriously limits its practical relevance;

b   that a critical appreciation of organizational storytelling will help you to develop a richer and more faithful appreciation of the dynamic processes that shape our organized worlds; and

c   that this knowledge of how the world (actually) works will help you to pursue purposeful intervention in your organization.

Take a few moments now to record the rhetorical projections that circulate commonly within your organization.

Upon what claims do these rhetorical projections depend?

Could these projections survive Chomsky's relocation exercise?

Am I suggesting, then, that stories have the capacity to shape our under-standing of social organization in ways that will have a bearing upon the prac-tice of (cultural) management? Yes!

Am I suggesting that stories are sure-fire success mechanisms that will allow you to take charge of what others, think, feel and do? Hardly!

My intention here is to demonstrate the manner in which an appreciation of organizational storytelling processes may be used to allow you (a) to develop and (b) to articulate an approach to leadership and management which in recognizing his-tory, context and plurality, works with rather than against the lived experience of social organization.

Accordingly, the remainder of Chapter 1 will proceed as follows:

We begin with reflections on the nature of organizational culture. Here, as we shall see, the 'definitions' of culture which circulate among managerial cadres are, in truth, nothing of the kind.

In an attempt to develop an account of organizations-as-cultures that can sustain critical inquiry, and in so doing support practical endeavour, we will consider a number of 'exhibits' (or, if you prefer, quotations) drawn from an eclectic range of sources. These exhibits we will array to explore, both, the historical complexity of cultural formations and their dynamism.

'Culture', as we shall see, is too often represented as a form of collective mental programming which imprints itself upon our thoughts and actions. Challenging this programming metaphor, we will demonstrate that the suggestion that culture is somehow the 'software of the mind' simply fails to concede the extent to which the software that supports our technological systems is prone to failure! Further-more, and perhaps more pertinently, we will show that the culture-as-software metaphor acts to deny what our own experience of the social world has taught each of us: that cultural proscriptions are, in truth, fluid and negotiable.

Having secured an appreciation of 'culture', which is rooted in an apprecia-tion of complexity and plurality, we will turn to consider the nature and pro-cesses of organizational storytelling. We will demonstrate that the assumptions which traduce culture as a metaphor of/for social life act similarly to diminish the practice of organizational storytelling.

Challenging the reduced account of organizational storytelling that has been placed before management practitioners we will re-view the organized world, *warts and all*, so that we might come to recognize our friends, our colleagues and our customers as actors with agency; as living, breathing, functioning, if flawed, adults within a managerial landscape, which, because it has been shaped by 'popular management', is prone to infantilization.

Getting to grips with culture

Deal and Kennedy (1982: 4) who were, together with the likes of Peters and Waterman (1982) and Pascale and Athos ([1981] 1986), pioneers in the field of 'popular management' (see Collins, 2013; 2020) offer, perhaps, the most concise account of organizational culture. They suggest that culture may be condensed to

Take a few moments to list the 'popular management' books that you currently own or have read.

How do these texts constitute the world of work?

In what way do these texts represent and account for the contemporary problems of management?

Can you recall any stories from these texts? If so please jot these down now?

Are there any aspects of your daily life or your work experience omitted or occluded by these texts?

a simple statement of fact. Culture is, they assert, simply 'how we do things around here'.

This is, of course, rather a long way from 'a definition of culture' but this statement does at least demonstrate a useful intuition about *what* people do at work and *why*. Thus the shorthand of Deal and Kennedy suggests that culture *is a pattern of action*, which is to say that we can come to know cultural norms and organizational values through sustained reflection on what people say and do.

In addition, the analysis developed by Deal and Kennedy makes it plain that 'culture' is also to be regarded as *a pattern for action* insofar as behaviours and policies express interests, priorities and matters of concern that shape our conduct, whether or not we choose to acknowledge this fact.

In this regard the cultural *norms* visible, for example, in the manner in which people dress, and in the terms they use when they address one another, reflect *values* as to what is useful and proper. In turn these *values* reflect a core set of *beliefs*.

To offer a general example of the relationship between norms, values and beliefs: Belief in the God of the New Testament should lead you to hold values associated with 'neighbourliness' and 'reciprocity' such that your conduct will demonstrate that you meet friends and strangers on the same terms, offering to all others the courtesy you would, yourself, hope to receive.

Parker (1993: 4–5) captures both faces of culture rather well in his account of the speech patterns that shape conduct and interactions in the city of Belfast. Noting the religious and political divisions, more-or-less opaque to outsiders, which shape daily life in Belfast, Parker reminds us that the *patterns of action* we observe underpin *patterns for action* that shape how the people of this city think, feel, act and indeed interact:

> If you are Protestant and 'British', you'll always call the second biggest city in Northern Ireland 'Londonderry': if you're Catholic and/ or Nationalist, you'll only refer to it as 'Derry'. Nationalists and Catholics speak of 'the North', Ireland or, intentionally aggressive, 'the Six Counties'. 'Northern Ireland' and 'Ulster' are Protestant terminology: and to speak of 'the Province' in front of a Nationalist is provocative, even if it wasn't intended ... Catholics and particularly Republicans never talk about 'the Troubles' – they use the blunter 'the war' or 'the struggles'. Even in the *minutiae* of pronunciation there are giveaways: the Department of Health and Social Security's initials are pronounced DHSS by Protestants, but by Catholics 'D Haitch SS'. So too with the IRA: more correctly 'The Provisional IRA', its members are only called the 'Provos' by Protestants: to Republicans, Nationalists and Catholics they're 'the Provies'; the slightly changed sound with its more moderating softness perhaps revealing something else as well. These are only some of the more obvious pointers. But in every conversation there'll come the faintest of suppressed grimaces, or the slightest flicker in the eye is a 'wrong' word is used revealing you to be one of the 'others'.

Who are the 'cultural insiders' within your workplace?

Are you an 'insider'?

If you are an 'insider' who is on the outside?

Who is 'the other' within your workplace and why?

Why do such divisions arise and prevail?

To answer this question would require a rather lengthy history lesson beyond the scope of this text *and* beyond the capability of the author. But the broad question remains, and indeed remains worthwhile because it reminds us that Deal and Kennedy's focus upon the 'here and now' (albeit with an eye to the future and with an agenda for change) tends to gloss over significant questions that arise in connection with:

a   the formation of cultural values and modes of expression;
b   the reproduction of social norms; and
c   the interests which these serve.

Given Parker's recognition of 'the other', therefore, it may be useful to observe that the 'definition' of culture, of what gets done and who/what matters, outlined by Deal and Kennedy, works best and, in truth, serves only privileged actors: the comfortable insiders whose interests and connections shape the 'mainstream' and in so doing tend to mark conflicting and/or contesting ideas as 'counter-currents', as 'minority interests' or, worse, nostalgic accounts of a world now passing into irrelevance.[2]

Schein's (1985: 6) account of culture is, perhaps, more elaborate than that detailed by Deal and Kennedy (1982). He argues that the term culture 'should be reserved for the deeper level of *basic assumptions* and *beliefs* that are shared by members of an organization, that operate unconsciously, and that define in a basic "taken-for-granted" fashion an organization's view of itself and its environment' (original emphasis).

This assertion is, of course, useful at one level. It is, for example, plain that we do not generally spend much time thinking about the orientations that shape our day-to-day interactions. As Burrell (1997) observes, we tend to think *with* rather than *about* our beliefs!

Equally Schein's account of culture reminds us that the *patterns of action*, which we are able to observe within the workplace (for example) do tend to be rooted in fairly deep-seated *patterns for action*, which in embodying beliefs and values act to set priorities, and so define what is 'good', what is 'bad', who is 'in' and who is 'out'.

Yet Feldman (1986) argues that Schein's work is deeply flawed because in locating the very foundations of our cultural lives in 'the unconscious', Schein moves the analysis of 'culture' from the observable social realm to the psychologist's couch. Noting the manner in which a focus upon 'the unconscious' acts to obfuscate the concepts and processes which merit more critical, analytical reflection, Feldman (1986: 87, original emphasis) complains that, despite its widespread use and application within the field of management, Schein's approach uses 'one of the most misunderstood concepts in the social sciences'. Thus Feldman warns us that 'the term "unconscious" does not refer to a place, but is a linguistic device to *describe* not *locate* mental phenomena'.

Hofstede's (1980) approach to 'culture' has a similar surface plausibility. Yet on closer reflection, Hofstede's approach, like that of Schein's, also reveals very deep flaws.

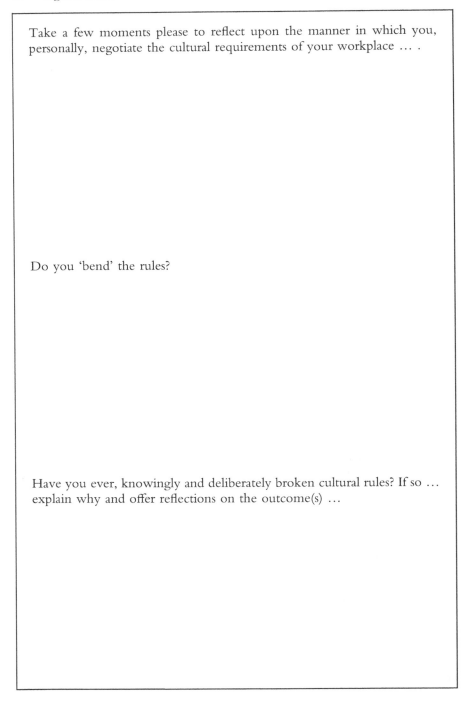

Take a few moments please to reflect upon the manner in which you, personally, negotiate the cultural requirements of your workplace ... .

Do you 'bend' the rules?

Have you ever, knowingly and deliberately broken cultural rules? If so ... explain why and offer reflections on the outcome(s) ...

Hofstede suggests that culture is a form of collective mental programming; the software of the mind. This allusion to software and the related suggestion that culture amounts to a form of collective mental programming does, of course, highlight the manner in which cultural ideas and cultural values are, to a considerable extent, commonly held and expressed. Yet those who have studied culture in the absence of an agenda to channel and to change what people, actually, think and do, generally remind us that 'culture' does not imprint our conduct or inscribe our behaviour. Instead, freed from the top-down agenda of 'managing cultural change', social culture tends to reveal itself as something which, while it is developed *historically* and maintained *socially*, is nonetheless negotiated *individually*.

Kuper (1993) captures this process, albeit in a tone that for a 'woke' generation may now appear just a little insensitive. Commenting upon Malinowski's pioneering studies in social anthropology, Kuper observes that despite the assertion that 'Culture is King', the Trobriand Islanders would routinely attempt to evade the reciprocal obligations, which Schein and Hofstede would suggest are somehow written in to our unconscious, mental coding.

Countering the suggestion that culture acts as a sovereign power, therefore, Kuper (1993: 24–25) suggests that an appreciation of context is key to the unlocking culture: 'whenever the native can evade his obligations without loss of prestige, or without the prospective loss of gain, he does so, exactly as a civilised business man would do'.

Collins (1998: 119) offers a similar, if more biographical, rendering of the manner in which Hofstede's software of the mind may be, variously, spliced and/or over-written. Thus the little deviant confides:

> In each of our own lives we can all, I am sure, find instances of … cultural renegotiation and modification. For example we might 'fiddle' our expenses, or 'fiddle' an insurance claim perhaps because the company is 'fair game'. We may, in spite of legal and religious prohibitions, and in spite of the frowns of our elders, argue that fiddling the company is acceptable because this form of individual action against a large company is not regarded as being 'real' theft in our eyes. Equally we may choose to procure resources from our place of employment (pens, stamps, a desk, a computer) based upon a similar understanding that such actions should not really be considered as theft. However, and in spite of such acts of theft, we probably regard ourselves as up-right, law abiding and, culturally speaking, mainstream.

Scott (1987) takes this a step further – without resorting to either autobiography or thievery. Indeed he offers a particularly intriguing account of the manner in which cultural ideas mutate as they are reproduced. Thus Scott suggests that actors, even in cultures marked by pluralism, may choose to give voice to culturally rooted declarations which they know to be bogus!

Commenting upon the relationship between Rwanda's Tutsi and Hutu peoples, Scott (1987: 50–51, original emphasis) observes that the pastoralist Tutsi, who were the feudal lords over the agriculturalist Hutu, pretended

Take a few moments, now, to record your reflections on a time when you felt obliged to 'put on a show' at work ...

How did this make you feel?

How do you feel about this now?

publicly that they lived entirely on fluids; the milk and blood products taken from their herds. This narrative, they believed, made them appear more awesome and disciplined in the eyes of the Hutu. And yet, despite this narrative, Scott observes that the Tutsi did, in fact, rather enjoy meat and ate it surreptitiously whenever they could:

> Whenever their Hutu retainers caught them *inflagrante delicto* they were said to have sworn them to secrecy. One would be astonished if, in their own quarters, the Hutu did not take great delight in ridiculing the dietary hypocrisy of their Tutsi overlords. On the other hand, it is significant that, at the time, the Hutu would not have ventured a public declaration of Tutsi meat-eating and the public transcript [that is the official, public, version of the truth] could proceed *as if* the Tutsi lived by fluids alone.

In your own life I am sure that you can find similar instances when you (or others around you) have voiced ideas and sentiments, which even if they are not quite bogus, are nonetheless rather a long way from the truth. For example, my experience suggests that when new or prospective clients visit your workplace, you and your colleagues will 'put on a show'; you will make a special effort to be chummy; you will, if my experience is any guide, set aside your differences to suggest a relationship other than that which prevails on a day-to-day basis.

We can see similar forms of play-acting at a national level. For example the people of Scotland generally protest that they are not at all racist. And most of my countrymen and women are, I accept, not racist. Nonetheless it is true that when Mark Walters, a black English-born player, signed for Glasgow Rangers in 1987, the supporters of opposing clubs within Scotland launched bananas on to the field of play.

Writing for the *i* a daily, national, newspaper (2019), Dr Punam Krishan, a Glasgow-based GP, offers a more contemporary account of life in Scotland. She observes:

> In my clinic a patient who had seen me from a distance told my receptionist that they wanted to see a 'Scottish doctor', judging me by my colour.
>
> My receptionist put them right, demonstrating to the patient that we had a zero-tolerance policy, that we are all equals and that their comments were not appreciated.

Dr Krishan, however, concludes on a more positive note which demonstrates that at least some of the Scots who voice such racist sentiments may be redeemed: 'The patient had no choice but to see me because I was the only doctor available. We established a great rapport and they have seen me several times since' (33).

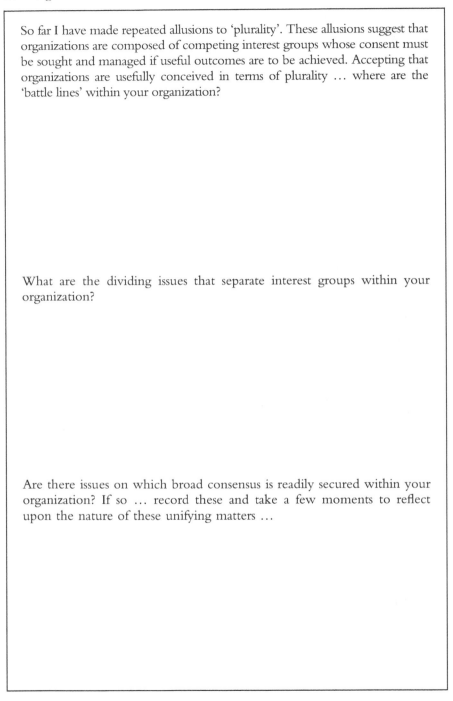

So far I have made repeated allusions to 'plurality'. These allusions suggest that organizations are composed of competing interest groups whose consent must be sought and managed if useful outcomes are to be achieved. Accepting that organizations are usefully conceived in terms of plurality … where are the 'battle lines' within your organization?

What are the dividing issues that separate interest groups within your organization?

Are there issues on which broad consensus is readily secured within your organization? If so … record these and take a few moments to reflect upon the nature of these unifying matters …

Martin (1992: 3) offers an analysis of culture which addresses many of the concerns raised in our discussion so far. Thus Martin's summary of 'culture' highlights the significance of plurality and history. Indeed her account of culture advises that we should take care to reveal and to acknowledge the manner in which forms of thinking and patterns of speaking become crystallized as cultural norms. These cultural norms may reflect privilege and may, indeed, entrench prejudice, nonetheless they will be, as Martin reminds us, open to (re)interpretation and, as our reflections on storytelling will make plain, vulnerable to subversion:

> As individuals come into contact with organizations, they come into contact with dress norms, stories people tell about what goes on, the organization's formal rules and procedures, its informal codes of behaviour, rituals, tasks, pay systems, jargon, and jokes only understood by insiders and so on. These elements are some of the manifestations of organizational culture. When cultural members interpret the meanings of these manifestations, their perceptions, memories, beliefs, experiences, and values will vary, so interpretations will differ – even of the same phenomenon. The patterns of configurations of these interpretations, and the ways they are enacted, constitute, culture.

Yet despite Martin's insights it would be fair to say that the analyses of 'organizational culture' that have been prepared for managerial leaders, and for policymakers more generally, are seldom properly embedded within an account of historical matters that reflects and respects the social dynamics of our organized lives.

Why is this so? Why are texts on 'culture' and the need to secure change in culture so blind to the realities of daily life?

Marxist scholars tend to suggest that 'being' determines consciousness. I doubt the wisdom of this suggestion because it is, I find, rather difficult to establish a determinate relationship between one social factor and another. Nonetheless it would be fair to suggest that 'popular management' texts are prepared for elite audiences, and so reflect the concerns and orientations of an elite that is, despite claims to the contrary, inclined to view employees as 'the other'; as troublesome variables who need to be made aware that their reflections and concerns are rooted in a worldview that is neither current nor pertinent.

This desire to change the cultural norms and values of 'the other', I suggest, tends to produce declarations on culture and cultural life that are myopic and, narrowly, self-serving. These declarations, we should note, operate both within and beyond work organizations.

For example, John Major, when he was British prime minister in the early 1990s, offered reflections on the cultural values shaping life on the collection of islands that is, too easily, reduced to the United Kingdom. Unveiling a 'back to basics' campaign at his party's annual conference in the autumn of 1993, which he hoped would save his failing government, Major publicly lamented the decline of (as he saw it) the old British values of neighbourliness, decency and courtesy.

Are you familiar with Orwell's novel *Coming Up For Air*? If John Major's nostalgic projection intrigues you, you may wish to read this book: It was I suggest Major's inspiration – whether or not he was consciously aware of this fact!

Vaunting these (fading) values, Major offered the party faithful nostalgic reflections on village greens and old maids bicycling to church. Yet Major's cultural reflections were as bogus as they were self-serving for they failed to acknowledge that British life is, and has been for a considerable time, both urban and secular. By the early 1990s, therefore, Major's cherished villages were populated by commuters and their churches were largely empty.

Furthermore, Major's nostalgia elides the cultural differences that divide the component parts of the UK. Thus Major's 'back to basics' agenda chose to ignore the fact that much of what we take to be quintessential of British culture is, in truth, a projection of (a) English[3] ideals and (b) governmental policies that were imposed upon the population.

The historian A.J.P. Taylor captures this imposition rather well within a passage that is worth quoting at length:

> Until August 1914 a sensible law-abiding Englishman could pass through life and hardly notice the existence of the state, beyond the post office and the police man. He could live where he liked and as he liked. He had no official number or identity card. He could travel abroad or leave his country for ever without a passport or any sort of official permission. He could exchange his money for any other currency without restriction or limit. He could buy goods from any country in the world on the same terms as he bought goods at home. For that matter a foreigner could spend his life in this country without permit and without informing the police. Unlike the countries of the European continent, the state did not require its citizens to perform military service. An Englishman could enlist, if he chose, in the regular army, navy or the territorials. He could also ignore, if he chose, the demands of national defence. Substantial householders were occasionally called on for jury service. Otherwise only those helped the state who wished to do so. The Englishman paid taxes on a modest scale: nearly £200 million in 1913–14. The state intervened to prevent the citizens from eating adulterated foods or contracting certain diseases. It imposed safety rules in factories and prevented women and adult males in some industries, from working excessive hours … Still, broadly speaking, the state acted only to help those who could not help themselves. It left the adult citizen alone. All this was changed by the impact of the Great War. The mass of the people became, for the first time, active citizens. Their lives were shaped by orders from above; they were required to serve the state instead of pursuing exclusively their own affairs. Five million men entered the armed forces, many of them (though a minority) under compulsion. The Englishman's food was limited and its quality changed, by government order. His freedom of movement was restricted; his conditions of work prescribed. Some industries were reduced or closed, others artificially fostered. The publication of news was fettered. Street lights were dimmed. The sacred freedom of drinking was tampered with: licensed hours were cut, and the beer watered by order. The very time on the clocks was changed. From 1916 onwards, every Englishman got up an hour earlier than he would otherwise have done, thanks to an act of parliament. (Taylor, 1979: 5–6)

Wright (1994) notes that the Hawthorne Studies were pioneering insofar as they were amongst the first to apply the concept of 'the social system' to the field of organization studies. It is worth observing however that despite modelling the world of work as a social system the researchers involved in the Hawthorne studies struggled to give credence to the social actions which they observed in their research. Those employees, for example, who were observed to work in ways designed to smooth their earnings and in so doing to maximise their long-run income were (quite wrongly) dismissed as irrational agents who misunderstood economics!

Noting this dismissal of what is, in fact, a highly rational form of conduct, Wright suggests that the very earliest accounts of organization-as-cultures were hamstrung by a top-down orientation that made 'objects' of its 'subjects'. This tendency I suggest continues to this day. Can you recall a time when legitimate concerns voiced by yourself or by colleagues have been dismissed out of hand? If so take a few moments to document this ...

Taylor's historical analysis, therefore, makes it plain that 'English culture'; the manifestation of an enduring Englishness built on, and around, bizarre licensing hours; weak beer; British Summer Time; a complacent press; and taxation (to scratch the surface) did not emerge over time, organically and by tacit agreement, but were policy-driven changes imposed upon the general population by a parliament that was, we should note, unwilling to extend the franchise to women!

Moreover, Taylor's analysis makes it plain that the immigration policies which the little Englanders now active in Conservative Party politics have advanced (ostensibly) to 'take back control'; to manage our borders; to protect 'our' culture from foreigners is, historically and culturally, peculiar and – for me – deeply unwelcome.

Indeed it is worth pointing out that the quintessential image of Englishness, employed by Major, of the 'old maid bicycling past the village green on her way to church', is a product of the Great War; an outcome of the slaughter endured by the 'pals battalions'[4] and recognition of the widows and 'surplus women' who were left behind by the wanton carnage that was the First World War.

But it is not only historical myopia which limits the appreciation of 'culture' developed by and within 'popular management'. There is, as we shall see, a process of *bowdlerization* present within accounts of organizational culture and cultural management which tends to limit (and to censor) the manner in which speech and action at work are represented.

* * * *

Since the time of the Hawthorne Studies scholars of management have understood that work is important socially (Wright, 1994). Many of us, after, all meet our sexual partners through 'work'. Indeed many individuals subsequently cheat on their sexual partners thanks to the relationships which form and develop through workplace interactions.

Yet accounts of organizational culture – especially those focused upon the articulation of tools and techniques designed to secure culture change – seem to reduce us to joyless, sexless drones at work.

'Popular management' texts; those works developed ostensibly to enable managers to effect changes in culture, assert that they have utility because they allow their readers to understand how people think, feel and act at work. And yet these texts seem to suggest that all we ever do is work, quietly; interrupting the silence only to chant the company's vision statement and its value proposition!

This (unwarranted) focus upon serious matters and instrumental concerns may be why the sociologist C. Wright-Mills (1973) suggested that those who would know of the world of work should consult with novelists and with poets rather than with organizational theorists. These men (and women) of letters, Wright-Mills suggests, respect their subjects and so understand better than the sociologist and political scientist the complex and fluid relationships that develop in and through 'work'.

Imagine for a moment your organization or your immediate work group as a TV *Sit-Com*. I don't imagine that this will be difficult. Take a moment now to reflect upon your colleagues ...

Building upon this reflection produce a brief descriptive cast-list for your daily drama ...

Can you think of an event that you might now develop into a small play?

When I read 'popular management' texts on 'culture' and 'change' in the light of the sociology of Wright-Mills I am struck by the absence of 'non-work'. Within 'popular management' no one skives. And no one laughs. Or I should say that no one laughs in that explosive, profane fashion that is truly infectious!

Moreover we should note that no one flirts. No one is ever angry, violent, envious, drunk or dishonest.

And no one ever curses.

I am not, of course, suggesting that I value or otherwise condone violence and/or drunkenness at work (or elsewhere). But I do wonder about the utility of supposedly 'practical' interventions which simply exclude these everyday behaviours from the analytical frame.

Managers are expected to manage processes which involve social interaction among *real* people. You agree?

And yet texts on the management of culture have 'cast lists' that contain few of the 'characters' we might expect to encounter in the workplace. Where, for example, is the (self-appointed) office joker with his 'hilarious' ties and matching socks?

Where is the reputed Lothario, who, of course, lives quietly at home with his mother?

Where is the 'family man'?

Where is the 'family man' who is nonetheless 'a bit handsy' after the second after-work drink?

Where is the woman with the troubled kids? And where is the smelly bloke with whom no one will share the lift?

I mean, can we take seriously texts which promise to unlock thought and to reprogram action in the workplace and yet exclude such 'stock characters'?

And how can we accept as practical advice the guidance of those who claim to be able to record, to take account of and to change patterns of speech and yet fail to acknowledge the single word, now so commonly employed, that it is, for many Britons, a form of punctuation?

I ask you: Is there any other field of endeavour or profession that would deliberately omit the central dynamic that shapes their work? I mean what use is a text on surgery that ignores the basics of anatomy?

And what use is a text on 'culture' text where no one *fucking* swears?

Can we hope to intervene purposefully in the organization; can we hope to change how people think, talk and act when at work when we simply fail to hear (and record) much of what they say?

* * * *

As we proceed we will offer an account of organizational storytelling designed to make space for those components of social and cultural life; the *fucking* 'imperfections' which 'popular management' would breed out of the workplace. To secure this, however, we must first pause to explain why it is that storytelling now needs to be recognized as being central to managerial work. Having established this (narrative) understanding of the nature of managerial work we will then consider the debates that define our understanding of storytelling.

Briefly − using bullet-points if you prefer − sketch out the argument outlined so far by this section of the workbook.

How and to what extent has this argument changed how you will now think about and speak of 'culture'?

Yet having reviewed this debate we will simply punch our way out of the wet paper bag that is this controversy to reveal the nature of that special narrative that is 'a story'. Having resolved this issue we will, then, consider 'story-types' before proceeding to offer a *pro forma* designed to assist you in the processes of character development and plot formation which you will develop in Chapters 2, 3 and 4 as you begin to craft your tales of work and working.

* * * *

The nature of managerial work

Following Fayol (1949), those who teach 'management' typically suggest that managers *plan, organize, command, control* and *co-ordinate* the actions of others. Moreover, those of us who teach 'management' tend to talk at length about the types of activity associated with these tasks. Yet we generally say much less about the practical problems; the social and political issues that arise when we seek to plan, to organize and to control the thoughts and actions of others.

In a small-scale but highly influential study Mintzberg (1973), however, offers a counterpoint to this abstract account and in so doing provides a useful appreciation of the day-to-day problems and dilemmas of managerial work. Managers, Mintzberg tells us, typically divide their time 80/20: They spend 20 per cent of their time working alone and 80 per cent of their time working directly and collaboratively with others.

Analysing these everyday interactions, Mintzberg reminds us that managers spend rather a lot of their working lives in meetings. Such meetings are, no matter how much we disparage them, vital, for it is when they are in such gatherings that managers are able to engage in forms of conversational exchange that are – to a greater or lesser degree – designed to engage people in forms of thought and action that they might otherwise choose not to pursue.

Mintzberg's analysis, therefore, reminds us that, despite the familiar codifications, which reduce *management* to an entity, a thing designed to command, to control and to direct, *managing* remains a human endeavour, a social-political process hinged upon the arts of persuasion. This expression, as we shall see, reflects an understanding that managerial control – the ability to shape the thoughts and actions of others – is incomplete. We should add moreover that managerial control is self-limiting.

Why is this so?

The short answer is that while the familiar codifications of management imply a fixation with 'command' and 'control', work necessarily implies co-operation. From this perspective, managerial work (and indeed the history of management studies) effectively condenses into a search for forms of co-ordination that do not break down or otherwise intrude upon the social co-operation that *gets things done*.

Edwards (1986) captures the tensions presented by managerial control strategies rather well. Reflecting upon the nature of the employment relationship,

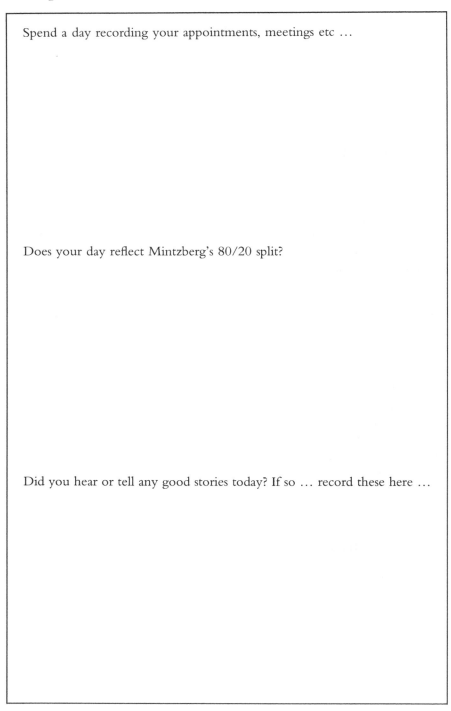

Spend a day recording your appointments, meetings etc ...

Does your day reflect Mintzberg's 80/20 split?

Did you hear or tell any good stories today? If so ... record these here ...

Edwards observes that 'labour' is quite unlike the other factors of production conventionally recognized in the study of economics. Thus Edwards observes that while we can simply purchase tracts of land and quantities of capital we cannot do the same with labour. Instead we are obliged to purchase 'labour power'; a capacity to work. The problem being, of course, that since most of us are paid simply to attend work, the capacity of labour power to do something useful, something profitable, may go unrealized.

Recognizing this indeterminacy, Edwards suggests that managers are obliged to find ways to direct and to control what their employees and co-workers do. Yet since employment is an exchange relationship, employees have an incentive to resist their employers' attempts, either to extend or to intensify their work activity.

This gap between the needs and orientations of the parties to the contract of employment suggests that the employment relationship is, at root, antagonistic. Moreover we would do well to note that this potential for conflict is built into the very foundations of the relationship. Thus Edwards warns us that the employment relationship which managers must steward is founded upon, and may be considered to be, a 'structured antagonism'.

It is also important to note, however, that the contract of employment is not simply an economic exchange. The contract of employment is not simply an agreement on the price of labour. It is, if you care to look carefully, also a document that traces and expresses the social and political controls, which shape our actions within and beyond the workplace. Discussing Britain's industrial revolution, for example, E. P. Thompson ([1963] 1972) documents the development of a complex penal code designed to punish certain forms of conduct deemed to be undesirable in the workplace. Weighing the merits of the 'five dollar day' which was implemented by Henry Ford, Beynon (1979) takes this analysis a step further and draws our attention to the broader social controls that employers have attempted to enforce within the contract of employment. Thus Beynon observes that Ford paid this very attractive daily rate only to those employees who had received a favourable report from the 'sociological department' on their family lives and on their broader personal habits!

The extension of 'management' beyond the workplace and into the family lives of employees demonstrates, paradoxically, the self-limiting nature of managerial control. Thus we would do well to note that Ford's 'five dollar day' and the snooping consequent on this award, was instituted because attempts to control and to direct the activities of workers by means of the moving production line had precipitated a quit rate in excess of 400 per cent per annum!

* * * *

Bendix ([1956] 1963) captures the self-limiting nature of managerial control. In a classic and often-cited passage (well, I cite it fairly regularly!) he offers the following observation: 'Management no matter how expert, cannot set out in advance exactly what must be done under all circumstances and how, but must rely to some extent on the workers' co-operation, initiative and experience' (256).

Spend a few moments unpacking the concept of the 'structured antagonism' ...

What does this term mean to you?

How do the dynamics of the employment relationship play out in your
organization? Do your policies smooth or exacerbate these tensions?

Recognizing that attempts to impose direct forms of control within the employment relationship are self-limiting, managers have, in recent decades, attempted to shift our common-sense understanding of the relationship of employment *from* a legal-economic exchange that is located within a contested setting, *to* a moral project.

Much of modern management practice has, therefore, retreated from direct control mechanisms and has, instead, focused upon narrative frameworks which assert that the parties to the employment relationship are agreed on organizational ends *and* means because all recognize that their mutual prosperity and survival depends upon vanquishing competitors and satisfying customers (see Collins, 2020).

Despite what you may have gleaned from 'Management 101', therefore, it should now be apparent that modern management practice is centrally concerned, not with control, but with 'talk', because the nature of the employment relationship means that those who have responsibility for the work that is undertaken by others are obliged to produce persuasive rhetorics that will convince colleagues, employees, shareholders and stakeholders that they are engaged in endeavours which are, in any sense, worthy.

So, what do managers do? They plan, they organize, they command, they control and they co-ordinate, of course. But it is purposeful talk that causes and allows all of these processes.

It is talk that persuades people to smile at the customer, to work hard, to stay late, 'to commit to change'.

It is talk that gets us up in the morning.

It is talk that keeps us moving.

It is talk that makes work meaningful.

It is talk that lifts our gaze from the vulgarities of economic exchange to embrace the nobilities of vision, purpose and mission.

In our next section we will look more closely at the purposeful talk, which is at the heart of managerial projects, as we consider the nature of organizational storytelling.

* * * *

Organizational storytelling

Our appreciation of what managers do is, nowadays, routinely located in 'talk'. Furthermore the purposeful 'talk' which is said to be central to managerial success has been structured, increasingly, as a form of storytelling. The reasons for this change are, in truth, complex and potentially contestable. Nonetheless I will attempt to offer a *précis* which, if not definitively true, is not demonstrably false.

In what ways and to what extent does your organization control and/ or impinge upon your conduct when you are not at work?

Take a few moments now to document your reflections here ...

As I see it the roots of our contemporary interest in organizational story-telling may be traced to two books which were published in the early 1980s. These books, *The Art of Japanese Management* co-authored by Pascale and Athos ([1981] 1986) and *In Search of Excellence* which was produced by Peters and Waterman (1982), share a number of common features.

Both texts were produced in an American economy which had been rocked by double-digit rates of unemployment, inflation and banking interest. Yet both texts also suggested that while America had become mired in recession the Japanese economy had continued to grow and, in market after market, had come to challenge the American dominance that, in the 1950s, had been assumed to be naturally ordained.

Capturing the scale of this challenge, Pascale and Athos ([1981] 1986: 20) offered the following observations:

> In 1980 Japan's GNP was third highest in the world and if we extrapolate current trends it would be number one by the year 2000. A country the size of Montana, Japan has virtually no physical resources, yet it supports over 115 million people (half the population of the United States), exports $75 billion worth more goods than it imports and has an investment rate as well as a GNP growth rate which is twice that of the United States. Japan has come to dominate in one selected industry after another – eclipsing the British in motorcycles, surpassing the Germans and the Americans in automobile production, wrestling leadership from the Germans and the Swiss in watches, cameras and optical instruments and overcoming the United States' historical dominance in businesses as diverse as steel, shipbuilding, pianos, zippers and consumer electronics.

Reflecting upon the roots of this remarkable economic success, Pascale and Athos suggested that Japan's growing dominance was, primarily, managerial. Japanese managers, the authors argued, had abandoned direct control mechanisms and in so doing had secured employee commitment to customers, to innovation and to change.

Pursuing this distinctive managerial capability, both Pascale and Athos and Peters and Waterman utilized the McKinsey 7-S framework. Drawing upon this *heuristic* they argued that American managers needed to re-balance the hard-S factors and the soft-S factors of business in order to ensure that American corporations would have cultures appropriate to the business needs of the 1980s and beyond.

Yet despite these very clear similarities only one of these texts has enjoyed broad commercial success.

* * * *

In Search of Excellence conceded that Japanese managers had achieved something remarkable. The Japanese, Peters and Waterman observed, had produced a competitive economy from the rubble of a society that we would do well to remember had, only 30 years previously, been the subject of nuclear attack. Twice!

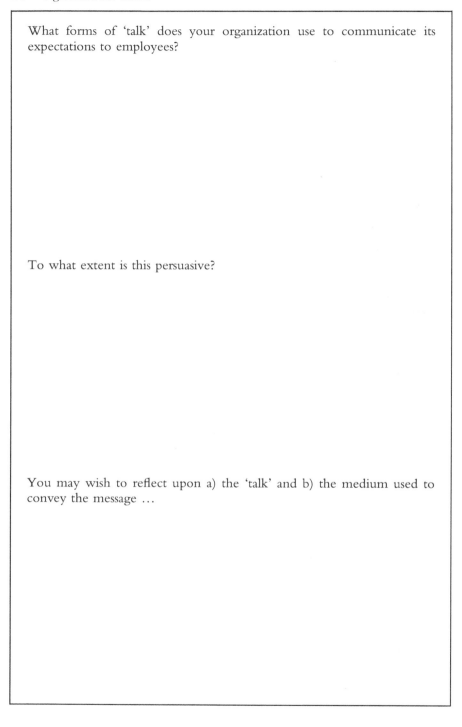

What forms of 'talk' does your organization use to communicate its expectations to employees?

To what extent is this persuasive?

You may wish to reflect upon a) the 'talk' and b) the medium used to convey the message ...

Yet *In Search of Excellence* insisted that there remained, within American management, real pockets of excellence such that rather than seeking, simply, to emulate the practices of their Japanese counterparts, American managers could learn from their home-grown contemporaries. Peters and Waterman, therefore, urged US organizations to develop a form of executive leadership, built upon the lessons available from America's best-run companies. This approach to management, they stressed, would be more than good enough to challenge Japan.

The text prepared by Pascale and Athos offered the careful reader a similar account of America's problems and suggested a broadly similar solution. However the title of this work and its focus upon what was taken to be remarkable about Japanese management encouraged more casual readers to form the opinion that *The Art of Japanese Management* simply vaunted Japan at America's expense.

In the mid-1980s I obtained my hardback copy of *The Art of Japanese Management* from a 'remaindered' book shop in Glasgow's city centre. At the same time *In Search of Excellence* was dominating the 'best sellers lists' (see Collins, 2007; 2020).

The relative performance of these books is, I believe, instructive. Despite the obvious symmetry of these texts, therefore, the 'success' of Peters and Waterman and the 'failure' of Pascale and Athos, should remind us that if you plan to place your dreams in the company of others you must be careful to construct a narrative that taps into the hopes, aspirations and fears of your intended audience. Get this wrong, offend or disappoint your 'discourse community', and your narrative will surely fail to make the emotional connections that will get things done!

Mindful of the need to connect with the expectations of their audience, Peters and Waterman essayed an account of 'change' that has become central to the narratives employed by 'popular management' (see Collins, 2020). Taking careful steps to avoid blaming America's managers for the country's economic slippage they argued that what had made America great in the 1950s – its hard-S capabilities – had placed it at a relative disadvantage in the 1970s because consumer preferences had altered to demand both quality and innovation (which Japan had delivered in spades!). In an attempt to secure a transformation in American management, therefore, Peters and Waterman argued that managers would need to learn from those organizations which had developed cultures dedicated to customers, quality and innovation.

Outlining the nature of the tools which would deliver such cultures, Peters and Waterman (1982) and later Peters and Austin (1985) urged managers to seek out and, where necessary, to create opportunities to model the forms of thinking and action that would be needed to deliver quality and innovation for customers. In short, Peters advised managers to develop and to cultivate stories which would create models for thinking and feeling and, *beyond this*, exemplars for action in contexts otherwise dominated by division and ambiguity.

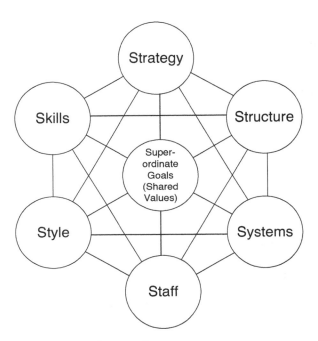

Figure 1.1 The McKinsey 7-S framework

John Steinbeck offers a useful illustration of the manner in which storytelling and shared talk, more generally, can be used to generate the sense of common purpose that is now central to the moral economy of managerial work.

In his short novel, *Of Mice and Men*, Steinbeck ([1937] 1974) constructs an unlikely and ill-starred friendship between two ranch-hands: Lennie, a small and quick-witted man, and George who remains, to all intents and purposes, a child in a giant's body. The extract reproduced below demonstrates the manner in which stories act to define our sense of self and our relationships with others. Thus it is worth observing that the tale that George and Lennie share demonstrates the difference between their partnership; their mutual endeavour and the lonely aimlessness of those who are, for the want of a dream made real by a shared story, doomed to spend the rest of their lives moving from place to place and working for others.

George, as we shall soon see, knows very well the story that he will demand to have performed. And yet he *needs* to have Lennie recite the tale.

George, of course, pleads that he retains this desire because he tends to omit key parts of the narrative, and so, fails to do justice to the tale. But these pleadings are, I suggest, false. The extract reproduced below gives us every reason to believe that George knows the story well and could render it fully. For me the truth of the matter is that George wants and needs Lennie to tell their shared story because this narrative acts like a contract and in getting Lennie to repeat the tale George can be confident that the covenant which forms their plan for a future hereafter still holds.

Steinbeck works hard, I have always thought, to ensure that we understand the significance of this tale and the manner in which it acts to solemnize a doomed undertaking between these unlikely friends. Thus as Lennie relents and begins to tell the tale, Steinbeck takes care to demonstrate that this story has significance precisely because it is so often repeated. As Lennie opens the tale for George and for us, therefore, Steinbeck tells us that his voice changes: It becomes deeper and the words flow rhythmically in a prayer-like fashion.

Our extract, of course, has a context. Every tale we announce is, if we are honest, in the middle of something else!

It is important to point out, therefore, that in the moments before our extract commences Lennie has been scolding George. Indeed the first time that we encounter this unlikely pairing Lennie is castigating his friend because he has been drinking from a stagnant pool.

George, it soon becomes clear, is always getting into some sort of trouble. And what is worse, Lennie, as the grown-up member of the partnership, has to resolve these difficult problems as they arise. As the novella begins, therefore, Lennie is already working on a plan to address the problems that generally develop when poor George is at large in the world of men.

Yet while George is innocent and alarmingly naive he is not entirely guileless. He offers no defence when Lennie scolds him for drinking from the pool, nor for all the other difficulties that he has visited upon the partnership. Indeed George accepts his culpability for the situation and volunteers to resolve both the immediate issue and Lennie's ongoing difficulties by going to live alone, like a hermit, in a cave.

Is there a tale that is familiar to you and which is commonly repeated within your organization?

If there is ... take a few moments to reflect upon why it is that this tale remains in circulation ...

Who knows this tale? Who tells this tale? Why?

Despite the fact that, when criticized, George routinely threatens to adopt the life of a hermit, Lennie quickly relents. Sensing a small, personal, advantage in this retreat George seizes his opportunity and demands that Lennie recounts the story that defines and brings purpose to their deep and enduring friendship:

> 'A'right, I'll tell you, and then we'll eat our supper ...'
>
> George's voice became deeper. He repeated his words rhythmically as though he had said them many times before. 'Guys like us, that work on ranches, are the loneliest guys in the world. They got no family. They don't belong no place. They come to a range an' work up a stake and then they go inta town and blow their stake, and the first thing you know they're poundin' their tail on some other ranch. They ain't got nothing to look ahead to.'
>
> Lennie was delighted. 'That's it – that's it. Now tell how it is with us.'
>
> George went on. 'With us it ain't like that. We got a future. We got somebody to talk to that gives a damn about us. We don't have to sit in no bar-room blowin' in our jack jus' because we got no place else to go. If them other guys gets in jail they can rot for all anybody gives a damn. But not us.'
>
> Lennie broke in. '*But not us! An' why? Because ... because I got you to look after me, an you got me to look after you, and that's why.*' He laughed delightedly. 'Go on now, George.'
>
> 'You got it by heart. You can do it yourself.'
>
> 'No, you. I forget some a' the things. Tell about how it's gonna be.'
>
> 'O.K. Some day – we're gonna get the jack together and we're gonna have a little house and a couple of acres an' a cow and some pigs and ...'
>
> '*An' live off the fatta the lan*',' Lennie shouted. 'An' have *rabbits*. Go on, George! Tell about what we're gonna have in the garden and about the rabbits in the cages and about the rain in the winter and the stove, and how thick the cream is on the milk like you can hardly cut it. Tell about that George'.
>
> 'Why'n't you do it yourself. You know all of it.'
>
> 'No ... you tell it. It ain't the same if I tell it. Go on ... George. How I get to tend the rabbits.'
>
> (Steinbeck [1937] 1974: 17–18, original emphasis)

Most managerial commentators, I suspect, would now accept that stories such as that cherished by George can help individuals to forge the emotional bonds, the common understanding and the spirit of co-operation that *gets things done*. But we should not confuse a superficial agreement on these matters with a deep and abiding consensus. Indeed we must be clear that the academic field concerned with organizational storytelling is scarred by debates which actively contest both the nature of stories and the organizing capability of these narratives.

We may begin to explore this terrain through a comparison of 'sensemaking' and 'sensegiving' perspectives on organizational storytelling.

Sensemaking and sensegiving perspectives

Sensemaking accounts of organizational storytelling often draw their inspiration from the work of Karl Weick (1993; 1995). Weick has become a leading figure in the study of management and organization, in part, because he offers a distinctive account of the dynamics of managerial work which places stories at the very centre of organizational life.

Weick argues that, on a day-to-day basis, each of us is obliged to navigate our lives under conditions that are marked by complexity and ambiguity. To reduce the complexity and to filter the ambiguity that threatens to engulf us, Weick suggests that we are obliged to construct personal narratives that situate and explain our problems, our emotions and our ambitions. Furthermore he suggests that – having constructed these narratives – we then tend to navigate our lives *as if* these constructs represent neutral, dispassionate observations of an external reality.

For Weick, therefore, social life and social action are, despite appearances to the contrary, constructed in and through narratives. What gets done, he suggests, is whatever has a good story.

* * * *

Weick suggest that good stories are grounded in reality. Yet these stories are driven by plausibility rather than by simple facts.

In an attempt to explain this understanding of the conditions of our organized existence, Weick (1995) considers the social construction of 'battered child syndrome'. Through this reflection Weick is able to demonstrate the essential distinction between 'interpretation' and 'enactment' and the role that storytelling performs in the constitution of sensible environments.

* * * *

Battered child syndrome

Thanks to a number of high-profile and, frankly, appalling court cases which have examined allegations of child neglect and physical harm, the idea that children might be injured or even killed by those who have been entrusted with their care is now rather familiar. Weick (1995) however reminds us that 'battered child syndrome' is actually a very recent medical-legal diagnosis. Consequently he is keen to trace the process of narrative formation and identity construction, which make 'battered child syndrome' a sensible explanation of events that have not been witnessed directly.

Weick asks: Why was 'battered child syndrome' once apparently unthinkable amongst medical practitioners?

The short answer is that 'battered child syndrome' remained, literally, unthinkable for so long as alternative, plausible, explanations for the injuries reported by children were allowed to endure.

Pursuing the processes which sustained the pretence that children would not be assaulted by the adults charged with their care, Weick suggests that medical doctors were inclined to co-construct case histories for childhood injuries refracted through the lens of their own childhood experiences. Thus Weick suggests that, having come from homes that were, for the most part, stable and nurturing, medical doctors were inclined to co-construct narratives which insisted that the young people who had been brought to their surgeries had been harmed through accidental events. These children were assumed to be loved but reckless; cared for but clumsy.

Thus a combination of (a) deceitful parents/carers who were prepared to offer false case histories and (b) medical practitioners willing to cultivate narratives that sought congruence with their own identities, rather than with more troubling forms of evidence, rendered systematic child abuse, more or less, unfathomable.

* * * *

Through his analysis of 'battered child syndrome' Weick reminds us that we do not simply 'interpret' events. Rather we 'enact' events within environments shaped by our own identities. In this respect 'battered child syndrome' was rendered unthinkable in so many emergency rooms because it conflicted so severely with the ideas, orientations and experiences of medical practitioners.

Yet Weick is also keen to point out that, beyond this elite, others within the medical establishment – radiographic technicians who were subordinate to and altogether less privileged than the clinicians – were inclined to enact alternative sensible environments that made 'assault' a plausible diagnosis.

Radiographic materials – x-ray photographs – are important in the enactment of these newly abusive environments for they allowed the radiographic technicians to challenge the case histories constructed by the clinicians. Thus Weick suggests that the radiographers were able to observe the primary complaint that had brought the child to the doctor, say a fractured arm, *and* perhaps just visible on the edge of the photographic plate, older injuries that had partially healed, say fractured ribs. Observing that these secondary injuries had not been reported and had, therefore, remained untreated, the radiographers were able to challenge the established pattern of sensemaking (the child is clumsy but cared for): If the parents in the waiting room were truly the loving guardians of a clumsy or reckless child how could they have failed to notice cracked ribs? Why would the loving parents developed in and through the clinician's narrative fail to seek treatment for the sort of incident that could cause fractured ribs?

Indeed if the parents were truly caring and loving why would they have failed to report the weeks of obvious pain and discomfort that is experienced when cracked ribs heal?

Is there a 'springboard story' within your organization?

If there is, take a few moments to reproduce this tale here …

What gives this tale its springboard characteristic?

If there is no 'springboard story' … why is this the case?

Does your organization need a 'springboard story' to address a persistent issue or problem?

Weick's account of battered children and narrative sensemaking is important in our analysis of culture and storytelling because it demonstrates that the tales we use (a) to describe our lives and (b) to situate our experiences and actions are rooted in identity. For Weick, therefore, who we are and what we do represent narrative achievements. We are, in a very real sense, therefore, actors in dramas that we have co-written.

Sensegiving accounts of organizational storytelling (see Gioia and Chittipeddi, 1991) build upon and yet modify Weick's analysis of social life. Thus sensegiving accounts of storytelling suggest that *since* all of us are obliged to construct our lives narratively and *since* action in organizations stems from such narrative constructions, managers *should* intervene in organizational processes in order to craft stories designed to enact their preferred goals. The problem being that sensegiving accounts of storytelling (like top-down accounts of culture) miss most of the drama, and so, tend to presume that managers can, fairly readily, produce purpose and direction for their employees through stories.

Esler (2012) captures the essence of this sensegiving approach. Yet he, at least, acknowledges the very real efforts required to sustain stories in contexts shaped by politically laden ambiguities.

Esler suggests that managers can *make things happen* through storytelling. He is, however, also keen to point out that this outcome will materialize only so long as the tales, crafted and rendered, have been designed to colonize the consciousness of the audience:

> The secret weapon of storytellers throughout the centuries has been to create a story which sticks in the mind, just as a successful musician will write a pop song with a melody so powerful that you cannot get it out of your head. Germans call this an *Ohrwurm*, literally an 'earworm', or 'earwig', which won't stop wriggling whether you like it or not, until it worms its way into your brain. Successful leaders work hard at creating an 'earwig', or they employ others to do it for them. They spend a lot of time wondering how to communicate their leadership story and subvert the counter-stories told against them.
>
> (Esler, 2012: 19, original emphasis)

Denning (2001) offers a concrete illustration of Esler's argument. In *The Springboard*, Denning confesses that he had tried and failed to convince his colleagues of the virtues of a key infrastructure project designed to bring clean water to the villages and homes of those living in the developing world. He observes, however, that nothing – not charts, or reports, or statistical analyses – would move his colleagues until he happened upon a tale, which in grim but deeply human terms, illustrated the effort that women and small children in parts of Africa have to exert, daily, in order to collect and to carry water. This story, Denning tells us, acted as 'a springboard' since it demonstrated to the audience present that very small children are, too often, denied the opportunity of an elementary education because they are obliged to spend most of each and every day collecting water.

Reflecting upon this tale, Denning argues that his story acted as a 'springboard'. It acted, he tells us, as an emotional lever for action because it demonstrated to those

Where do you come down on the debate – as I have described this –
between Denning and Peters?

Take a few moments now to explain your rationale ...

who remained unmoved by logical argument and rational calculation that something *should* be done. And perhaps more importantly this tale showed that something *could* be done to resolve this dreadful situation.

Taken together, Esler's 'earworms' and Denning's 'springboard stories' suggest that stories have a capacity to:

- tap emotions;
- shape understanding;
- precipitate action.

Indeed it is worth observing that Denning's 'springboard story' *does things* because it plants and propagates narratives, which humanize events and, in so doing, makes real, problems which had hitherto appeared to be merely abstract or somehow far-removed from other more pressing or more local concerns.

In later sections we will examine the manner in which sensemaking accounts undermine the sensegiving narratives preferred by Denning and indeed by 'popular management'. Yet before we move on we should make it plain that not all those who would endorse a 'sensegiving' account of storytelling actually agree on what stories can do within the workplace.

* * * *

Tom Peters (see Peters and Waterman, 1982; Peters and Austin, 1985) places storytelling at the very core of managerial work. Indeed, for Peters, storytelling is essentially synonymous with managing. Those who would get things done, Peters insists, need to craft and share narratives that will allow others to understand that what needs to be done is, in truth, useful and worthy.

Denning accepts much of this argument. Yet he seems to suggest that stories perform an ancillary organizational function, and so, exercise their effects only at key junctures. Thus where Peters suggests that 'talk' is what managers (should) do all day and every day, Denning seems to insist upon a separation between 'talk' and 'action'.

For Denning, therefore, springboard tales are useful as projects commence or stall because they can help to engender a common sense of purpose. But springboard stories, Denning insists, will not dig wells. At some point, he argues, the talking needs to stop and the digging needs to start. Peters, however, would find it difficult to accept this. Indeed he would counter that Denning's attempt to separate 'talk' and 'action' is wrong at a conceptual level and wrong-headed at a practical level, not least because managers need to sustain and, periodically, will need to repair and/or renew the moral projects that they are obliged to construct in and through stories. Thus Peters would tend to argue that, at some level, stories actually do dig wells!

For the record: I am inclined to agree with Peters on this issue. Yet to leave our discussion on this point would be to overlook the divisions that persist *within* sensemaking accounts of organizational storytelling. To allow an exploration of these divisions we will consider what Greatbatch and Clark (2005) have referred to as 'elaborate', 'terse' and 'inductive' or 'audience-centred' (see Collins, 2013; 2020) accounts of storytelling.

In deference to John Steinbeck I have developed a test – *the George and Lennie Test* – for organizational storytelling. Take an organizational story that is familiar to you and reproduce it here ...

Now ask: to what extent does this tale retain a capacity to construct and to sustain a mutual endeavour? This, in a nutshell is *the George and Lennie Test*.

If the story selected 'passes' the test ... on what basis does it pass?

If it fails ... why does it fail?

And could you, now make changes to improve the functionality of the story?

Attempt This Challenge in the Space Below

Elaborate, terse and inductive approaches to storytelling

The 'elaborate' account of storytelling is, for students of organization, perhaps most closely associated with the work of Gabriel (2000; see also Collins, 2018). Gabriel argues that poetic or proper stories are special forms of narrative which possess core structural characteristics. He suggests that stories:

- involve characters in a predicament;
- unfold according to a chain of events that reflects (a) the structure of the plot and (b) the essential traits of the characters involved;
- call upon symbolism/symbolic matters;
- indulge poetic embellishment and narrative development;
- have an arc which moves the reader/audience from a beginning through a middle section to a successful conclusion;
- seek a connection not with simple facts but with local understandings and/ or more general truths.

Boje's (1991; 2001) 'terse' alternative to the 'elaborate' narratives preferred by Gabriel captures many of the points detailed above.

Accounting for the presence of storytelling in our everyday lives, Boje takes his cue from Weick (1995). He observes that, on a day-to-day basis, each of us confronts a key problem: how to make sense of a 'complex soup' of ambiguous and half-understood problems, events and experiences. Reflecting upon this problem of ambiguity, Boje suggests that people are obliged to construct and retrace their lives, retrospectively, through stories. He warns us, however, that we must distinguish 'stories' from 'narratives' if we are, fully, to understand the richness of organizational sensemaking.

Narratives are, Boje (2001: 1) warns, plotted, directed and staged to produce a linear, coherent and monological rendering of events, while 'stories are self-deconstructing, flowing, emerging and networking, not at all static'. In an attempt to provide an alternative to these monologues of business endeavour Boje introduces the concept of the 'antenarrative'.

For Boje (2001), 'antenarrative' has two faces. On one face, Boje's focus upon 'antenarrative' is based upon the assertion that 'stories' precede 'narrative'. Thus, Boje suggests that stories are 'antenarrative' insofar as they come before the processes of staging and directing, which, as he sees it, lead to the development of 'sequential, single-voiced', top-down 'narratives'. On the obverse face, Boje calls upon the rules of poker and suggests that an 'antenarrative' represents 'a bet' (or 'an ante') that retrospective sensemaking may emerge in the future from 'the fragmented, non-linear, incoherent, collective and unplotted' (1) stories, which come before corporate monologues.

This 'antenarrative' approach overlaps to some degree with the account offered by Gabriel (2000). In common with Boje, Gabriel observes that stories offer local and intimate accounts of situations, events and predicaments. Furthermore, Gabriel concurs with Boje that it is, vitally, important to distinguish 'stories' from other 'narrative' forms. Yet at this point the accounts of storytelling prepared by Boje and Gabriel diverge quite fundamentally.

Gabriel, as we have learned, insists that stories are special forms of narrative with definite, structural characteristics. Boje, however, adopts a rather different approach which seeks to redefine the very nature of organizational stories. In an initial move, Boje (1991) suggests a 'terse' approach. Thus he suggests that, within the conversational give-and-take of storytelling *in situ*, the four words which announce 'you know the story' are actually equivalent to telling a poetic tale. Later, in a more radical move, Boje (2001) suggests an 'antenarrative' account which, as we have seen, suggests that stories should be regarded as those special forms of narrative that exist *prior* to the crystallizing processes of casting and plotting.

I consider David Boje to be both a supportive friend and a senior colleague. Yet we disagree on these points. Thus, I (see Collins, 2018) protest that while the so-called 'terse stories' observed by Boje represent invitations to recall, either, a pattern of events or a particular rendering of a tale, they are not, properly speaking, stories, for they lack the resources necessary to construct the common purpose and the shared identity apparent in our account of George and Lennie. Similar concerns apply to Boje's (2001) antenarrative conceptualization of organizational stories.

Boje's suspicion of narrative monologues, as we have seen, stems from a concern that academics and business commentators have been, altogether, too keen to endorse a simplistic 'sensegiving' account of storytelling (see Gioia and Chittipeddi, 1991) and have, as a consequence, colonized the organizational world with tales that are linear, single-voiced and top-down in their orientation. Noting the practical consequences of such sensegiving accounts, Boje (2001) suggests that we should be suspicious of corporate plotting and should, in an attempt to free ourselves from such hegemonies, embrace antenarratives, which, as the name suggests, come before the crystallizing processes of plot formation. Yet a 'tale' which proceeds in the absence of a plot device and characterization (see Collins, 2007; 2013; 2018) amounts to a failed story; a projection that breaches the covenant formed between the storyteller and her audience. I am therefore unconvinced by the utility of Boje's antenarratives.

* * * *

Reflecting upon the stories rendered by the gurus of management, Clark and Greatbatch (2002) review the 'elaborate' account advanced by Gabriel (2000) and the 'terse'/antenarrative model advanced by Boje (1991; 2001) and reject both. Advancing their preferred alternative, they counter that their 'approach is not to conceive of a story as a performed entity which is transmitted by a storyteller but rather as a performative activity whose emergent character is dependent upon in situ behaviours of the participants and whose meanings may vary across contexts' (155).

Building upon this account of audience dynamics, Greatbatch and Clark assert that both the 'elaborate' and the 'terse' approach to storytelling are flawed because they proceed from an account of storytelling that is structural in character, and so, predicated upon 'a priori formal definitions' (110) of narrative form. Thus for

Greatbatch and Clark (2005) stories are defined, not by narrative form, but by public proclamation: 'The gurus have to indicate that they are about to tell a story so that the members of the audience hear what is being presented as a story' (110).

Yet Greatbatch and Clark (2005) acknowledge that success in storytelling depends upon the continuing consent of the audience. They are, therefore, immediately obliged to qualify this statement. Thus they add that any segment of talk that is announced as a tale must also be 'recognizable and hearable as a story' (110).

There are, however, serious methodological difficulties with this approach: If stories are defined in the social space that remains between the speaker's proclamation and the audience's reaction, how can Greatbatch and Clark be sure that what the gurus choose to announce as 'stories' have, in fact, been recognized and heard by the congregation in these terms?

The short answer is that the authors cannot and choose, simply, to ignore this issue. Thus despite their rejection of Gabriel's elaborate model, the approach preferred by Greatbatch and Clark actually depends upon the assumption that they know (a) what the audience can hear, (b) what the audience can recognize and (c) what the audience will choose to define as a story. Thus the observation that 'Peters told 12 stories' (Greatbatch and Clark, 2005: 112) in the seminar performance(s) reviewed by the authors makes sense *only* if we accept that Greatbatch and Clark can know in advance what an audience might find 'hearable' as a story. Yet the authors rule out this presumption. Indeed they insist that any attempt to define stories *a priori* and in relation to their narrative form would be high-handed and deterministic!

Recognizing that the 'terse'/antenarrative approach developed by Boje (1991; 2001) and the 'inductive', or audience-centred, approach preferred by Greatbatch and Clark (2005) reject and yet require the Gabriel's 'elaborate' model the remainder of this section, and indeed the remainder of this workbook, will adopt a classical or structural approach to storytelling.

To advance our appreciation of this classical account our next section will reflect upon what it is that distinguishes 'stories' from the other related narrative forms that, as Boje quite correctly observes, are too often confused.

* * * *

Reports, opinions and proto-stories

In this section we will consider narrative types. We commence by contrasting 'stories' and 'reports'. In addition we will utilize the *pro forma* (reproduced verso) in order to encourage reflection upon the narrative components that are necessary to build and to sustain 'epic', 'comic', 'romantic' and 'tragic' tales within your workplace.

* * * *

Gabriel (2000), I believe, would probably concede that 'stories' and 'reports', storytelling and *reportage*, often overlap. Nonetheless he suggests that it is helpful to consider (and to maintain) the analytical distinctions which separate 'reports' from 'opinions', 'proto-stories' and 'poetic tales'.
Please do use the pro forma to aid your storytelling.

This story is about a time when:

The underlying theme of this tale is:
(Is this, for example, a tale about 'commitment', 'loyalty', 'loss', 'luck', 'insecurity', 'inequality' …?)

The person(s) reading/hearing this tale should feel:
(Is this a funny story? Will the audience feel pride, warmth, shame …?)

Hero/central character:

Assistants:

Predicament:

Agency:

Motive:

Credit:

Fixed qualities:

Notes for subsequent draft(s)

(This is where you reflect upon your next steps and what, now, needs to be done to improve the tale. Do you, for example, need to 'flesh out' the hero and his/her motivations? Does the predicament, perhaps, need fuller explanation/contextualization? Is your hero truly worthy of the emotional response you wish to solicit?)

Reports

Alan Sillitoe[5] (1979: 9), a respected English novelist, writing before the days of 'fake news' and 'alternate facts',[6] has observed the manner in which facts and fictions blur and are indeed combined by storytellers to secure dramatic outcomes:

> everything written is fiction, even non-fiction – which may be the most fictional non-fiction of all. Under that heading are economic reports, international treaties, news items, Hansard accounts, biographies of 'great people', historical blow-by-blows of crises and military campaigns. Anything which is not scientific or mathematical fact is coloured by the human imagination and feeble opinion.

Gabriel, I suggest, would accept this. Yet he is nonetheless keen to corral these narrative forms in separate pens.

Pursuing the analytical boundaries that separate stories from reports, therefore, Gabriel argues that reports are monological in character. Reports, he insists, invite factual verification whereas stories reflect, in Sillitoe's (1979: 9) words, 'a pattern of realities brought to life by suitably applied lies'.

* * * *

Opinions

Opinions are similar to stories. Both may, for example, contain factual and symbolic materials. However Gabriel's (2000) analysis suggests that 'opinions' seek to 'tell' rather than to 'show' the audience what has happened. Consequently 'opinions' may lack the qualities of seduction necessary to convince others that the events under scrutiny are fully relevant to their concerns or, somehow, consonant with their experience.

* * * *

Proto-stories

Classical formulations of the poetic tale (see Aristotle, 1965) suggest that stories develop an interaction between scene, actor and plot that proceeds to a satisfactory conclusion. In this respect, 'proto-stories' may be considered to be proto-typical of poetical tales insofar as they contain some but not all of the elements necessary to the development of a story. Thus proto-stories may have some level of characterization but will remain incomplete and broadly unsatisfactory because, for example, they lack a plot device that can deliver a useful ending. In this regard proto-stories represent 'stories-under-construction' inasmuch as future rehearsal, character development and/or embellishment may produce those missing elements that make the proto-typical narrative unsatisfactory in its raw and undeveloped form.

* * * *

Poetic tales

Poetic tales are, as we have seen, similar to 'reports' insofar as both narrative forms will contain or convey 'facts'. Yet where 'reports' exist ostensibly to convey 'facts', poetic tales will embed such certainties within narratives that seek a connection with larger or more general truths.

Facts of course matter to storytellers and may need to be addressed directly within the narratives they construct. But such facts cannot be allowed to intrude upon the preferred arrangement of narrative resources. If empirical facts dominate, the story will become, simply and blandly, a 'report' and, as Sillitoe (1979: 9) reminds us, the 'laws of fiction' dictate that a tale that gets too close to *the* truth 'loses its air of reality'.

Frédéric Beigbeder's (2005) fictionalized account of the terrorist attacks that are, nowadays, reduced to the term '9/11', identifies the dilemmas identified by Sillitoe and in navigating, usefully, the dividing line between narrative forms, offers a useful illustration of the manner in which authors may combine 'fact' and 'fiction' in search of deeper and more abiding truths.

* * * *

Beigbeder's tale builds upon the known facts of the 9/11 attack. Yet it cannot be read as a report because the narrator speaks to us from beyond the grave!

This dead man's story takes place in the 'Windows on the World' restaurant located on the 107th floor of the north tower and deals with the certain fate of all those present that morning at 8:46am: 'You know how it ends; everybody dies. Death, of course, comes to most people one day or another. The novelty of this story is that everyone dies at the same time in the same place' (Beigbeder, 2005: 1).[7]

But we do not and cannot know in detail what happened during the 105 minutes that elapsed between the first impact and the collapse of the second tower. Beigbeder's story fills this space. It re-imagines the terrifying events of 9/11 through the eyes of a young man and his two children, Jerry and David, who were until 8:46 am 'at the top of the world' (3).

'Hell lasts an hour and three quarters', Beigbeder tells us. 'As does this book' (6).

There are certain 'facts', of course, that Beigbeder cannot ignore. Dates and times are, as the extracts reproduced above demonstrate, central to this 'tragic' tale. Indeed we should note that Beigbeder (2005: 11) pauses to offer a pretty detailed note on the construction of the towers:

> Under the watchful eyes of the Rockerfeller family and the supervision of the New York Port Authority, the Twin Towers were imagined by architect Minoru Yamasaki (1912–1982) and Associates with Emery Roth and Sons. Two concrete-and-steel towers 110 stories high. Almost 10,000,000 square feet of office space. Each tower boasts 21,800 windows

and 104 elevators. Forty thousand square feet of office space per floor. I know all this because it's my job in some sense. Inverted catenary of tri-angular cross-section measuring fifty-four feet at the base and seventeen feet at the apex; footing 630 feet; steel lattice columns on the thirty-nine-inch centers, weight 320, 000 tons (of which 13, 357 tons is concrete). Cost: $400 million. Winner of the Technological Innovation Prize from the National Building Museum.

Yet, Beigbeder's account of this morning in New York is not a report: It deals artfully (if painfully) with matters, processes and events unknown. And it culminates with a scene that, according to the official report, simply did not happen. Thus we should note that while bodies were seen to fall from the towers, the official transcript insists that no one jumped. To countenance the possibility of jumpers is, apparently, to dishonour those who died.

Beigbeder, however, is a novelist. Whatever the 'facts' say (and these *are* open to dispute), Beigbeder is at liberty to invite a different reading of those seen to 'fall':

> Since David died, Jerry won't let go of him, cries on his cold forehead, strokes his closed eyelids. I stand up take him in my arms, a little prince with blond, lifeless hair. Jerry reads my thoughts, he shudders with grief …
>
> Just before we jump, Jerry looks me straight in the eyes. What was left of his face twisted one last time. It wasn't just a nosebleed anymore.
>
> 'Will Mom be sad?'
>
> 'Don't think about that. We have to be strong. I love you honey. You're one hell of a kid.'
>
> 'I love you too, Dad. Hey, Dad you know what? I'm not scared of falling – I'm not crying and neither are you.'
>
> 'I've never known anyone as brave as you, Jerry. Never. You ready buddy? On three …'
>
> Our mouths gradually distorted from the speed. The wind made us make curious faces. I can still hear Jerry laughing, holding tight to my hand and to his little brother's, plummeting through the heavens. Thank you for that last laugh, oh Lord, thank you for Jerry's laugh. For a split second, I really believed we were flying.
>
> (Beigbeder, 2005: 295–296)

Take a few moments, now, to remind yourself of the structural components of a 'story' …

List and explain these components …

If you can, take a few moments to write about the ways in which these
components need to interact to produce a pleasing narrative …

Let's take a moment to pull ourselves, and the threads of our analysis, together:

- Stories are, perhaps, the primary means by which we come to terms with the world.
- The stories that we tell others, and indeed ourselves, act to filter the complexity of our worlds and in so doing reduce the ambiguity that would otherwise engulf us.
- Stories draw upon 'symbolic resources' as they seek a connection, not with cold hard facts, but with the larger truths which emerge from the artful interweaving of facts and fictions.
- Stories indulge embellishment and invite a consideration of thoughts, feelings, sights, sounds, light and shade that would probably be unwelcome in 'reports'.
- While our actions and our identities are shaped by the stories we tell (and hear), our stories remain local, organic and polyphonic in character.
- The intentions of the storyteller (and we might add the *rapporteur*) may be subverted by audiences disinclined to accept the plot, characterizations and/or moral advanced.
- Poetic tales challenge the excesses advanced by the proponents of 'cultural engineering': They assert, proudly, their plurality, their polyphony, and in so doing they demonstrate the capacity to redeem and to retrieve those patterns of speech; those experiences, emotions and voices silenced within 'popular management'.

Sillitoe (1979: 7–8), for me, effectively summarises these bullet points (and the analytical issues they convey) in the opening passages of *Raw Material*:

> As a boy I walked into the middle of Nottingham, passing St Barnabas' Cathedral on my way down Derby Road. In a deep niche of its grey-black wall sat a man with no legs, selling matches. The niche had a heavy wooden door to it, and he could lock the place securely every night before going home.
>
> At the time of packing up I saw him, put the money into his pocket without counting it – as if he had already noted every penny that dropped there during the day. Then he folded the mat and set it at the back of the niche with his stock of matches. After a look to see that everything was tidy he came on to the pavement and locked the door. He propelled himself down the road by his two hands, the trousers of his brown suit pinned under his trunk. He wore a collar and a tie, which somehow saddened his look of respectability.
>
> His brown eyes watched people walking by all day long, and his single great indisputable truth was that the rest of the world had legs. He was privileged in having such an enormous and satisfying fact all to himself, but what a price he had to pay for it. His features were a prison wall that held his thoughts and everything he suffered. He smiled but never talked.

His fate did not seem so terrible to me as I now think it was. He had a way of earning a living, shelter from the rain while doing it, and a fact about himself with which he could gainsay every other truth. I did not envy him, but in my simplicity as a child I realised that his truth would have been absolute if only he had given into it entirely by staying in his wall-cave during the night as well.

When I asked my parents how he had lost his legs my mother said he'd been run over by a tram as a boy. My father told me they had been blown from under him twenty years before at the Battle of the Somme. My grandmother heard he'd been born like that. Grandfather Burton thought it as a good way to dodge his share of proper work.

It was difficult to know which of these tales to believe, but they ceased to matter after a while.

Reflecting upon the indulgences granted to storytellers, such as Sillitoe, Gabriel (2000; 2004) draws our attention to the 6Fs of narrative construction.

The '6Fs' of narratives

Gabriel (2000; 2004), as we have seen, insists that 'stories' and 'reports' need to be separated analytically. Reporters are required to chronicle events. A reporter, for example, might *tell us* that the sun was shining in New York on the morning of 9/11 and might, for example, list the air temperature, the barometric pressure and the mean wind speed.

A storyteller, however, would reveal all of this by *showing us* (for example) the sun reflecting on the windows of the towers; the play of light on the Hudson River.

Consider for example the manner in which Trumbo ([1939] 1994: 1–2) portrays the declaration of war in 1914 … and its aftermath:

> World War I began like a summer festival – all billowing skirts and golden epaulets. Millions upon millions cheered from the sidewalks while plumed imperial highnesses, serenities and other such fools paraded through the capital cities of Europe at the head of their shining legions.
>
> It was a season of generosity; a time for boasts, bands, poems, songs, innocent prayers. It was an August made palpitant and breathless by the pre-nuptial nights of young gentlemen-officers and the girls they left permanently behind them. One of the Highland regiments went over the top in the first battle behind forty kilted bagpipers, skirling away for all they were worth – at machine guns.
>
> Nine million corpses later, when the bands stopped and the serenities started running, the wail of the bagpipes would never again sound quite the same.

* * * *

To achieve a poetic effect such as that achieved by Trumbo, storytellers may need to rearrange characters, situations and events in order to secure the attention and the ongoing affiliation of their audiences. Pursuing this crucial distinction between *reportage* and storytelling, Gabriel (2004) tells us that poetic tales call upon one or a number of (6F), factors. Namely:

- Framing
- Focusing
- Filtering
- Fading
- Fusing
- Fitting.

Framing

Stories are not simple assemblies of events nor are they collections of fact. They are, instead, artful constructions; careful arrangements of plots and characters.

Beigbeder's (2005) tale works (for me) for example because he (re)frames the events of 9/11 through the eyes of a father and his two children.

We cannot really know what happened on the 107th floor, of course, but we can, with Beigbeder's help, begin to imagine what those who were present felt and did in the aftermath of the attack. Indeed Beigbeder's *framing* of 9/11 is shocking and horrifying *and yet* edifying because, caught in the horror of the moment, the central character acts in a truly heroic fashion. He does not, it is worth noting, go all *Diehard* on us.

Beigbeder's 'leading man' does not crawl through ventilators. He does not kill terrorists. And he does not lead his compatriots to safety.

Instead, Beigbeder's hero puts his faith in the Fire Department. Yet while he waits, vainly, for rescue, he takes steps to protect his children from the creeping reality that (we know) will kill all those present:

'Dad, did the plane crash into the tower, Dad, WHASHAPPENINGDAAD?'

'No, of course not', I smile. 'Don't worry, boys, it's all special effects, but I wanted it to be a surprise: it's a new attraction, the plane was a hologram – George Lucas did the special effects, they do a false alert here every morning. Really scared you though, huh?'

'But, Dad, the whole place is shaking and, and the waitresses are scared and they're screaming ...'

'Don't worry they use hydraulics to make the restaurant shake, like they do in theme parks. And the waitresses are actors, they're just plants put in among the paying customers, like in *Pirates of the Caribbean!* Remember *Pirates of the Caribbean,* Dave?'

'Sure, Dad. So what's this ride called?'

'Tower Inferno'.

'Right ... Fuck, sure feels real ...'

'Dave, we don't say fuck, even in a towering inferno, okay?'

(Beigbeder, 2005: 60, ellipses in original)

* * * *

Focusing

The practices associated with the second F-factor, Focusing, overlap to some degree with the account of Framing outlined above insofar as the development of a particular focal point, necessarily, limits the extent to which we may for example allow a frame that acknowledges the existence of other actors and/or other concerns. Thus it should be clear that the decision to focus upon the 'Windows on the World' restaurant means that, from our position atop the north tower, we cannot see the events of 9/11 from the perspective of the firefighters and first-responders who ran into the towers as other fled. That said, Beigbeder's all-seeing narrator does include (the last moments of) a firefighter.

Turning his attention to 'Jeffrey', an employee of the restaurant where the children and their father had been enjoying breakfast, Beigbeder captures both the nobility of these ordinary people and the futility of their situation:

Jeffrey is looking for water, but nothing comes out of the faucet anymore, so he tips water out of a vase hanging from the ceiling to moisten his group's napkins [to allow them to breathe]. He tears down the red drapes to staunch, or at least to filter, the smoke. He waves tablecloths out the window where huddles of people are screaming for help. Jeffrey isn't scared anymore. He's become a hero. He upends tables over puddles so his friends can cross the corridor without being electrocuted by bare wires dangling in the water.

He really did everything he could for the others before taking his chance. He wanted to put his idea to the test; maybe he was just tired of watching the people he loved die and being unable to save them. He grabs the four corners of a curtain (two corners in each hand) and jumps. At first the fabric billows like a parachute. His buddies cheer him on. He can see their petrified faces. He picks up speed. His arms have too much weight to carry, the curtain tangles. He'd been paragliding in Aspen, so he knows how to use updrafts. Even so he falls like a stone. I would have liked to be able to say that he made it, but people would simply criticize me for the same reason they criticized Spielberg when he had water gush through the nozzles in the gas chambers. Jeffrey didn't land gracefully on his toes. Within seconds his derisory piece of fabric became a torch. Jeffrey literally exploded on the plaza, killing a fire-fighter and the woman he was rescuing.

(Beigbeder, 2005: 206–207)

Recognizing the overlap between our first two F-factors I will now consider Gabriel's third and fourth F-factors – *filtering* and *fading* – together.

* * * *

Filtering and fading

Sellar and Yeatman ([1930] 1938) offer a satirical reading of English history that would now qualify as 'postmodern' in its sensibility. In their 'compulsory' prefacing statement they observe:

> Histories have previously been written with the object of exalting their authors. The object of this History is to console the reader. *No other history does this.*
>   History is not what you thought. *It is what you can remember.* All other history defeats itself.

(vii, emphasis in original)

* * * *

When Britons reflect upon the wars that defined the twentieth century (and their identity) they have, it seems to me, a tendency to adopt the historiography preferred by Sellar and Yeatman. Thus Britons engage 'filtering' processes and 'fading' mechanisms in order to (re)construct their history in a peculiarly self-serving fashion.

* * * *

Immigrants to the British Isles who wish to secure the right to permanent residence are now obliged to undertake 'citizenship' instruction and are, furthermore, required to pass an exam on British history and culture. As a 'subject' of the Crown I find the notion of a citizenship faintly amusing, nonetheless one of the questions in the exam, designed to assure competence in British culture and history, requires the would-be citizen to confirm that, in 1940, following the retreat of the army from Dunkirk, Britain stood *nearly* alone against Nazi aggression.

This assertion of Britain *nearly* alone, however, overlooks the fact the British military was, at this time, dependent upon the United States (then a neutral power) for much of its food and its war materials – and had obtained both on preferential terms!

Furthermore the notion of 'Britain *nearly* alone' overlooks the extent to which the British military machine included Poles; the Free French; American volunteers; Canadians; Australians; New Zealanders; Indians; Arabs; Fijians; Malayans; and Africans from a host of countries including The Gambia, Sierra Leone and the Gold Coast, many of whom, we should note, actually enjoyed residency rights in Britain until the mid-1970s (see Miles, 1982).

Writing for the *Guardian* David Lammy (2019) is exercised by the processes of filtering and fading which allow British history to be (re)written in a manner that – figuratively and literally – *whitewashes* our past.

Touring the military graveyards of Kenya, which are maintained (both home and abroad) by the Commonwealth War Graves Commission (previously the Imperial War Graves Commission), Lammy is struck by their order and under-statement. Yet as he looks at these regiments of white crosses he is struck by the fact that the names inscribed are familiar. The names are 'British'; these are the graves of Smiths; Wilsons; Cartwrights; Godfreys; Macdougals; Weirs …

Where, Lammy asks, are the African names?

Estimates suggest that between 100,000 and 300,000 African soldiers perished in the First World War.[8] Yet these men have been denied the dignity of a headstone and their families have been denied the solace of a grave because the then Chair of the Imperial War Graves Commission decided, frankly, that their sacrifice was not worthy of this lasting and final recognition.

So much for Britain alone.

So much for the publicly espoused British values of neighbourliness, decency and courtesy.

And who was this man, disinclined towards the decent burial of Britain's colonial subjects? Step forward the hero of the armchair warrior, the doyen of English nationalism, Winston Spencer Churchill.

* * * *

Fusing

Good storytellers understand those details that are central to their narratives. They also recognize those characters and events that are, consequently, marginal to the plot. In many cases the fusing processes which, variously, compress temporal differences or which act to remove characters from the stories rendered are fairly benign. Thus it is worth observing that when screenplays are developed from novels and/or factual accounts, events and characters are often cut to produce a cinematic experience that will not exhaust or otherwise try the patience of the audience.

John Berendt's ([1994] 2009) *Midnight in the Garden of Good and Evil* is a non-fiction work which deals with a murder. The book has been very successful, spending 216 weeks on the *New York Times* best-seller list.

In 1997, perhaps unsurprisingly, a film adaptation of this book, directed by Clint Eastwood, was released. This film, it is worth noting, cuts or combines many of the characters who feature in Berendt's book, reducing the original cast-list of 106 players by half!

* * * *

Fitting

Storytellers who refuse to *fit* their work around the expectations of their audiences may find that their tales are simply rejected by their audiences or, given the realities of the industry, by their publishers.

In *Stories for Management Success* I offered reflections on the manner in which John Steinbeck ([1942] 1983) had been obliged to rework *The Moon is Down* to reflect concerns raised against an earlier iteration of this tale. This example remains pertinent, however, it is worth observing that 'fitting' processes do not simply rotate on a geo-political axis. They also address matters, for example, pertaining to gender and class. Indeed, in this context it may be useful to consider the Bechdel test (sometimes known as the Bechdel-Wallace test), which has been developed to challenge the manner in which film-makers have been inclined to develop scripts which act to exclude women.

The Bechdel–Wallace test is named after the American cartoonist, Alison Bechdel, whom, we should note, credits the idea to her friend Liz Wallace. The test offers a measure of the representation of women in fiction and although it now exists in a number of variants generally asks three, core questions:

1   Does the work feature at least two women who talk to each other?
2   In conversation do these women talk about something other than a man?
3   Does the work identify these women by name?

The website Bechdeltest.com has drawn upon a database of some 6,500 films and in April 2015 reported that only 58 per cent of the survey passed these three tests. That said, it is worth observing that some have suggested that this 58 per cent pass-rate exists only because a strict reading of the Bechdel-Wallace test will offer films a passing grade even if they contain, for example, (stereotypical) conversations which depict two, named, female characters talking about marriage and babies.

Placing this methodological wrinkle to one side it may be helpful to observe that contributors to the news website *Voactiv* have observed that, taking 2013 as the base year, films passing the Bechdel-Wallace test have grossed $4.22 billion whereas those films flunking the test earned $2.66 billion.

As you prepare to tell stories in and of work you may be well advised to bear this in mind!

Gabriel's '6F' factors usefully convey the manner in which poetic license is exercised and employed. In our next section we will look more closely at the poetic tropes underpinned by the practices of framing fusing, fitting, etc.

* * * *

The poetic tropes

Just a few moments' reflection should reveal that not all stories are alike. Some stories make us laugh. Some make us cry. Others are designed to make us angry.

How do storytellers and, more importantly, how might you manufacture these outcomes within organized settings?

Gabriel (2000) argues that storytellers call upon 'poetic tropes' or generic attributions as they attempt to make events meaningful. Outlining these poetic tropes, Gabriel suggests that poetic tropes are the attributes which breathe life into stories, and so, give them the capacity to communicate experience. Poetic or proper stories, therefore tend to attribute:

1   Motive – which, for example, defines events to be accidental or incidental.
2   Causal connections – which outline the cause and effects of actions.
3   Responsibility – where blame and credit are allocated to actors and actions.
4   Unity – such that a group comes to be defined as such.

Take a few moments to highlight the ways in which Sillitoe's reflections uses:

● symbolism
● embellishment
● polyphony

to secure our understanding of the scene.

Now ... read the extract once more ... highlight, now, those things that Sillitoe *tells us* and those components of the scene that he *shows us* ...

5   Fixed qualities – such that heroes are heroic and villains, villainous.
6   Emotion – to describe the emotional characteristics of actions.
7   Agency – whereby volition is variously raised or diminished.

And finally, Gabriel draws our attention to:

8   Providential significance – which is especially important in certain tales, for example, where higher forms of being – Gods, angels, super-heroes and wizards – intervene to restore justice and order.

Gabriel observes that authors may structure the poetic tropes to produce a number of different 'poetic modes', designed variously to inculcate pride in, or to bring laughter forth from, the enraptured listener. Documenting the main poetic modes, Gabriel suggests that a tale may be (a) comic, (b) tragic, (c) epic or (d) romantic, depending upon the construction and organization of characters and events. It is important to note, however, that Gabriel's terminology departs, somewhat, from the traditional labels used to define storytelling tropes. Thus in the analysis of Shakespearean works, for example, 'comic' tales are those that conclude with an upturn in the hero's fortunes whereas 'tragic' tales conclude with a downturn in our hero's prospects. In contrast Gabriel's 'comic' tales are humorous in outcome and intent. Thus, for Gabriel, comic tales precipitate laughter whereas 'tragic' tales are said to generate sadness. 'Epic' tales, in contrast, typically concern the lives and endeavours of remarkable figures. Consequently these stories tend to have simple and rather linear plot-lines. Indeed epic tales often devote little time to the intricacies and complexities of character development. Instead these stories focus upon action, movement, achievement and closure as they encourage us to admire the achievements of the special individual who has been placed at the very centre of the drama (see Collins and Rainwater, 2005).

Before we can craft stories of organization, however, we need to consider in more detail the characteristics of the epic, comic, romantic and tragic forms as these are commonly constituted nowadays. In addition it is vital that we understand the manner in which narrative resources are arranged in order to conjure and to sustain these distinctive narrative forms.

* * * *

The arrangement of narrative resources

In an attempt to develop a concrete understanding of narrative form *and* an appreciation of the arrangement of narrative resources, required to create and sustain the epic, the comic, the romantic and the tragic form this section will consider a number of stories in outline. These brief reflections are intended to provide useful, practical guidance on the arrangement of narrative resources that you might apply to your own storytelling practices.

Take a few moments please to reflect upon a favourite or familiar epic tale ...

Please record the core components of this narrative below ...

The epic form

To illustrate the epic form I have chosen the graphic novel *Wimbledon Green*, by Seth (2006). Most readers, I assume, will not be familiar with this rather wonderful little book so I will spend just a few moments outlining its central *conceit* and its key characters. Before I do this however a few words on 'graphic novels' is perhaps merited.

To many people graphic novels are *just* comic books; the stuff of childhood and adolescence. They are, consequently, not to be taken seriously as works of art or indeed as 'literature'.

This perspective is understandable – if mistaken. After all comic books, or *comix*, even when they are beautifully illustrated, remain for most casual observers, a form of *juvenilia* focused upon 'superheroes' and beautiful if large-breasted female characters who just happen to wear skin-tight clothing *all the time!* Yet there is a segment of this market, dedicated to the production of what have come to be known as 'graphic novels'. These graphic novels, we should note, often address serious subjects; grown-up topics. Marjane Satrapi (2003), for example, has produced a graphic novel which offers an account of her childhood experiences of the Islamic revolution, which occurred in Iran in the late 1970s. Similarly Joe Sacco (2003) offers an account of the Palestinian *Intifada* which took place during late 1991 and early 1992. In addition we should also acknowledge Spiegelman's (2003) prize-winning Holocaust survivor-story.

Unlike these texts, Seth's *Wimbledon Green* does not deal with geo-political matters or with revolution. Instead it deals with the 'fan-boys', or worse, the *Stans* [9] who buy, share and trade *comix* while earnestly debating the merits of superhero 'multi-verses'.

Wimbledon Green, the eponymous hero of Seth's book, is a comic book collector. But he is no ordinary 'fan boy': He is the greatest comic book collector in all the world. He is also a mysterious character; a man surrounded by rumour, myth and innuendo. And like his glamorous contemporaries in the serious, fine art world, Green enjoys a fabulous standard of living: He lives in a palatial residence; is tended by a man-servant and travels, often, by private helicopter. Wimbledon Green is, in essence, a chubby Iron Man (stripped of the metal suit) combined with Indiana Jones!

Seth's *Wimbledon Green* adventure concerns our hero's attempts to locate and to acquire the most sought-after comic book in the world: 'Green Ghost #1'. Green, however, faces competition from other notable collectors who want this book *and* his status as the acknowledged number one collector.

Building upon a *pro forma* suggested by Gabriel (2000) *Wimbledon Green* may be read as an epic tale involving:

A hero: Wimbledon Green
A quest: The mission to acquire 'Green Ghost #1'.
Assistant(s): Mr Dozo, Green's man-servant, and Miss Flat-Iron, his counsel.
Protagonists: Green's rival collectors, namely: Waxy Coombs; Chip Corners; Nelson H. Bindle; 'Very Fine' Findley; R. Saddlestitch; Doc Astro; and Daddy Doats.

Take a few moments please to reflect upon a favourite or familiar comic tale ...

Please record the core components of this narrative below ...

In a (ig)noble quest that is built around:

A predicament: How to acquire 'Green Ghost #1', the most desirable comic book in the world (and other treasures) against rivals who are driven by a mixture of avarice and revenge.

To advance and sustain this tale we need to accept that comic book collectors inhabit a world where wealthy, mysterious individuals will criss-cross the country in search of treasures and will engage in underhand conduct to unearth and to secure, what we might with a nod to archaeology name, 'a hoard' of comic books. In addition we need to focus the attention of the audience upon:

Agency: Green is 'number one'. Yet he is a rogue and has in the past used a mixture of instinct, skill and low-cunning to best his rivals.
Motive: Our 'hero' is driven by a desire to possess rare and valuable books, of course, but he is also driven by the subsidiary desire to best his rivals.
Credit: This flows, primarily, to Green, who is a strategist and, consequently, master-of-deception.
Fixed qualities: Green is, of course, ruthless in his pursuit of comic books and in his desire to amass a personal hoard. Yet he is, in his own mind at least, a connoisseur and archivist who will secure and preserve what others (you and I) consider ephemera.

The successful arrangement of these resources leads to a conclusion, which sees Green best his rivals. As the narrative concludes, therefore, we find Green, once again, preparing for his next quest – wherever this may take him.

The comic form

To illustrate the comic form I have chosen the film *Scrooged*.

I have chosen this because, one way or another, I feel confident that you will know the story. Thus we should point out that *Scrooged* is a very, very funny re-telling of *A Christmas Carol*.

In this rendering of the classic Dickensian tale, Bill Murray plays Frank Cross, a youthful, ruthless and highly successful TV executive who cares little for the lives and responsibilities of those who must work for him. He has therefore scheduled – on Christmas Eve – a live, musical performance of *A Christmas Carol*.

Like Scrooge, Cross is a heartless and joyless businessman and, like Scrooge, he has a now deceased business partner and mentor. This mentor, Lew Hayward, visits Cross from beyond the grave to inform him that he must mend his ways if he is to secure happiness on earth and peace in the hereafter. In keeping with the original text, Lew warns Cross that he will be visited by three spirits who will show him the error of his ways. And, again keeping faith with the original, Frank Cross chooses to ignore this vision, explaining it away as a bad dream brought on by rich food.

Take a few moments please to reflect upon a favourite or familiar romantic tale ...

Please record the core components of this narrative below ...

Scrooged is, I must confess, one of my favourite films. It is very, very funny and while it is faithful to *A Christmas Carol* it re-imagines the tale in a truly inventive manner. *Scrooged* of course secures its impact upon me because of the manner in which it arranges its narrative resources. Thus it casts:

A misguided hero: Frank Cross, whom it is worth observing, is also the plot's rescue object.
Assistants: Lew Hayward, Frank's deceased friend and mentor, and the three spirits … whose coming has been foretold.

In a tale of comic misadventure which visits misfortune, indignity and ultimately redemption upon Frank Cross as it deals with:

A predicament: Frank is blocked; his ambition and his vanity have blinded him to the fact that, as Dickens tells us, mankind is his business. Indeed as the plot develops we learn that Frank is alone: he abandoned his girlfriend (and true love) Clare Phillips (played by Karen Allen) when she challenged him about his priorities. Furthermore his relationship with his only brother is cold and distant.

To reveal this problem and to secure Frank's redemption within a comedic frame, the film needs to shape our appreciation of our hero's character and predicament in terms of:

Agency: Frank Cross was, like Ebeneezer Scrooge, a lonely child. Ignored and unloved in childhood, Frank Cross has grown into a selfish, uncaring adult. And yet through flashbacks we learn that Frank was, previously, decent and friendly towards co-workers. Indeed it is important that we understand that Frank formed a deep and loving relationship with Clare. This relationship was of course cast aside yet its presence in Frank's life does at least demonstrate that he has qualities which make him worthy of our support and indeed worthy of redemption.
Motive: Redemption is, of course, the primary motive force: When we first meet Cross he is ruthlessly ambitious. Yet as the film progresses Cross is reminded that a different, a better, life based upon charity, compassion and love is not only possible but necessary.
Credit: Lew and the three spirits act as catalysts for a change in Frank's worldview and values but it is plain the primary credit belongs to Frank: Frank has seen the light. Frank has chosen a different path. The prodigal is returned … to humanity.
Fixed qualities: Frank is initially vain, ambitious and distracted from his purpose as brother, friend and lover. But his earlier life allows us to see that he was, as a young man, capable of love and worthy of love in return.

The romantic form

In my last major work on stories and storytelling (Collins, 2018: 57) I did not offer a concrete example of a romantic tale. Instead I offered an imagined romance, 'a stereotyped product of my prejudiced imagination' designed to lampoon many of the 'romantic tales' that have been produced for a mass-market audience. This was, I now realize, more than a little unfair. Not all romances are clichéd and hackneyed affairs. In an attempt to make amends I will essay a different approach in this workbook as I examine the film *Love Actually*.

Love Actually is, like *Scrooged*, 'a Christmas film' and while it has genuinely funny moments it is, at root, a romance. The film features many genuine stars, however it would be fair to suggest that the drama's central characters are played by Hugh Grant (who appears as the British prime minister) and Martine McCutcheon who plays, Natalie, a working-class woman employed within the 'household staff' of number 10 Downing Street (the official residence of the British prime minister).

Yet to focus our summary solely upon these two characters would be to overlook the manner in which the budding romance that develops (against the odds) between Natalie and the prime minister is woven into a tableau which includes no fewer than eight couples, three love-triangles; a budding pre-teen romance; the love between siblings; and, perhaps most touching of all, the realization of platonic love that endures between an otherwise lost, lonely and ageing pop star and his long-suffering manager.

Thus *Love Actually* might be rendered as a romantic tale that assembles the following elements:

A hero: Hugh Grant's prime minister is the film's focal point and its 'hero' for as he learns to love there is a prospect that Britain (at least) will become a better, more decent and compassionate place.

A predicament: The prime minister is new to his office. He knows that he is vulnerable before the media and his political rivals. Yet he is captivated by Natalie and she too is attracted to him. Separately, however, both understand that any match between them would be considered unsuitable. Will this curious couple allow their love to blossom?

To pursue this question to a satisfactory conclusion, *Love Actually* needs to indulge the artful arrangement of key narrative resources:

Agency: We learn from the outset that the prime minister, while obviously a statesman, is not at all stuffy and is, in truth, a decent and down-to-earth man. He is, for example, unfazed when an obviously nervous and working-class Natalie swears at their first meeting. Yet it soon becomes clear that the prime minister will need to overcome the proscriptions of the British class system and the restrictions associated with his office if he is to acknowledge his love for Natalie.

Motive: The prime minister wants to be true to his values but is restricted by the *Realpolitik* of international relations and is therefore required to compromise on his values. This state of affairs prevails, uncomfortably, until the president of the United States abuses his position to make an unwelcome pass at Natalie. This alarming event causes the prime minister to rethink his priorities. He is obliged to acknowledge his love for Natalie and the need to reconfigure relations with the United States.

Credit: The primary credit goes to the prime minister but, in truth, the film invites us to rejoice with all those who have found love, kept love or rekindled their love for one another.

Fixed qualities: Love is universal. Love conquers all.

Of course not all romances are simple (if agreeable) *schmaltz*. Some romance stories are more challenging and some end tragically. For example the film *Brokeback Mountain* which was adapted from a short story penned by Annie Proulx (2006) deals with the sexual and emotional relationship that develops between two, I was about to say 'cowboys' because in the movie they wear Stetson hats, but the truth is that the central male characters, Ennis and Jack, meet and fall in love when they are employed as shepherds.

Brokeback Mountain is a romance because it deals, frankly, with love and with all-too-human emotions. Yet it may also be read as a tragedy because Ennis and Jack find themselves in a context where they cannot publicly profess their love. Indeed, as the film develops, these characters are obliged to spend much of their lives trying to deny their identities and their sexualities, both, to themselves and to their spouses, their families and their communities.

* * * *

The tragic form

The final form I have chosen to discuss is the tragic form. Where the comic form is designed to precipitate laughter, and where the epic form is arranged to solicit pride and admiration, the tragic form is designed to generate feelings of sorrow and/or indignation (see Collins, 2018). The film I have chosen to illustrate the tragic narrative form is *The Empire Strikes Back*, otherwise known as *Star Wars: Episode V*.

This film, while it is the sequel to *Episode IV*, ends rather differently to its precursor. Thus while *Star Wars* concludes with the destruction of the Death Star and ends with laughter shared between the cast, *The Empire Strikes Back* visits new and potentially devastating problems upon our heroes.

Han Solo, we learn, is in debt to a gangster. During the film he is captured by a bounty hunter who delivers him to the gangster, Jabba the Hutt. Jabba punishes Solo — as a lesson to others who do not pay their debts — by having him frozen in 'Carbonite'.

Take a few moments please to reflect upon a favourite or familiar tragic tale ...

Please record the core components of this narrative below ...

Meanwhile Luke, who had previously embarked upon his training as a *Jedi knight*, has been drawn into premature combat with Vader. Luke (*spoiler alert*) learns that Darth Vader is his father and while he escapes from the duel with his life he loses a hand in the encounter. As the film concludes, therefore, the rebels are in full retreat.

Viewed in terms of our *pro forma* we have:

A hero: Luke Skywalker.
A quest: The need to free the galaxy from the yoke of an evil empire.
Assistants: Princess Leia; Obi-Wan Kenobi; Han Solo; R2-D2; C3PO; Chewbacca.
Protagonists: Darth Vader; Jabba the Hutt; Bobba Fett.

In a tragic tale which deals with:

A predicament: How to defeat the empire and in so doing return democracy to those world and peoples kept down by the empire.

To develop our appreciation of this predicament the film employs:

Agency: Luke and his confederates choose to fight on, despite the odds.
Motive: Freedom must be fought for and secured.
Credit: The rebels fail in their endeavours yet they remain worthy of our support and admiration for they fight for freedom, for self-determination.
Fixed qualities: The rebels love freedom and wish to live in peaceful co-existence with their allies. The Empire, however, craves power and will variously subjugate or annihilate whole worlds to secure its ends.

The successful arrangement of these resources produces a narrative that provokes feelings of loss and sadness among the intended audience, not to mention shock at the realization of Luke's parentage.

* * * *

You should now have a more developed appreciation of the ways in which narrative resources may be arranged to produce useful and meaningful outcomes. As you prepare to craft and share stories within your workplace you may find it useful to use some version of this *pro forma* to ensure that your storytelling (a) remains plausible, (b) consistent and (c) promotes the forms of thought and action that you would prefer.

In an attempt to assist you in your use of this *pro forma* and in your pursuit of useful narrative outcomes, Chapter 2 offers a series of maxims designed to help you to frame, focus and refine your storytelling practices. Yet before we embark upon this we must pause again to consider those stories which circulate from the bottom-up as we consider 'the uniqueness paradox'.

* * * *

The uniqueness paradox

This workbook commenced with an analysis of organizational culture. It conceded that organizations are usefully considered in cultural terms. Yet we have argued that those accounts of culture and cultural change which have been prepared for practising managers offer representations of the social world that are top-down in orientation. Such top-down accounts of culture, we have demonstrated, are ultimately unhelpful as guides to purposeful managerial intervention.

In an attempt to address these limitations, we have argued that an account of storytelling rooted within an appreciation of the dynamics of sensemaking offers a tool for understanding culture and, consequently, the tools necessary to craft an agenda for change. In this brief section we return to our opening concerns to offer an explicit acknowledgement of the manner in which stories carry and reveal cultural norms ... if you are ready to listen!

To this end we consider the uniqueness paradox in organizational storytelling and the stories – not told – within 'popular management'.

* * * *

Martin et al. (1983: 439) observe that most organizational cultures make a claim to uniqueness. They observe, too, that organizational members generally seek to substantiate this claim to uniqueness by referencing cultural manifestations such as stories. Yet Martin and her colleagues point out that the organizational stories, which they have encountered through their research, 'exhibit a remarkable similarity in content and structure'. There exists, they tell us, therefore a 'uniqueness paradox' in the sense that '*a culture's claim to uniqueness is expressed through cultural manifestations that are not in fact unique*' (439, original emphasis).

Examining organizational stories as cultural manifestations, Martin et al. argue that 'seven stories that make tacit claims to uniqueness ... occur, in virtually identical form, in a wide variety of organizations' (439).

To aid analysis of these seven story-types, the authors identify the tales as a series of questions which, in highlighting core anxieties in relation to the experience of work, narrate the organization 'from below':

1   Do senior organizational members abide by the rules that they have set down?
2   Is the big boss human?
3   Is the organization meritocratic?
4   Will I get fired?
5   Will the organization assist me to relocate?
6   How does the organization deal with mistakes?
7   How does the organization deal with obstacles?

These seven story forms, while not exhaustive of narrative possibilities, are, the authors argue, widespread *and* enduring because they 'express tensions that arise from a conflict between organizational exigencies and the values of employees, which are, in turn reflective of the values of the larger society'

(447). Indeed Martin et al. suggest that the story-types which arise in relation to the anxieties expressed in the questions above, circulate widely and are maintained within the memory of organizations because they project deep-seated concerns which organizational members have with respect to:

- Equality
- Security
- Control

Reviewing the relationship between these core anxieties and the seven story-types identified in and through their research, Martin and her colleagues argue that the stories developed in response to questions 1, 2 and 3 (above) deal with concerns related to equality and inequality at work. Stories developed in response to questions 4, 5 and 6, in contrast, relate to tensions formed around a security–insecurity duality. Finally, stories developed in response to question 7 reflect concerns with respect to control and autonomy in this context.

It is these tales I suggest that you need to seek out and to incorporate within your repertoire of storytelling. There are a number of issues that shape my suggestion that you should pay special attention to these tales as you attempt to come to terms with culture:

1   These tales are widespread in organizations.
2   These tales reflect the core and persistent anxieties which you and your colleagues must manage on a day-to-day basis. They are therefore the heartbeat; the background hum to your organization.
3   Many of these tales will be about YOU.
4   These tales are often ignored and/or devalued within 'popular management'. This is folly, however, for these tales offer *real* insights on the manner in which people actually think, speak and act within your organization.
5   These tales, from the bottom-up, provide a useful comparator for your own storytelling practice. If your preferred storyworld simply fails to countenance concerns which colleagues have with respect to 'security' for example you are simply going to fail when you attempt to 'reach out' through storytelling.

* * * *

It is worth reminding ourselves that the tales developed in response to the persistent organizational anxieties identified by Martin et al. (1983) and the questioning attitude which they precipitate, may be rendered in a variety of ways. For example a story rendered in response to the question '*Is the big boss human?*' might be rendered as a tragic tale.

In *Scrooged*, which we considered just a few moments ago, for example, Frank Cross has a long-suffering secretary named Grace. Grace is a single mother. Her partner was murdered and her youngest son has been rendered mute since witnessing the attack that killed his father.

Grace works hard to support Frank. Indeed in an early scene she can be seen fixing him a drink and adjusting his attire prior to an important meeting with a senior colleague. And yet, Grace is under-valued and unappreciated.

Frank Cross, for his part, is a man under pressure. He has invested a lot of his company's money in a live Christmas Eve performance and needs to ensure that this (a) goes well and (b) secures a large audience. As the performance date approaches, however, Frank begins to become concerned. At late notice he decides that he, now, needs to work late to manage his own rising sense of anxiety … and when Frank works late, Grace needs to do likewise.

Grace protests, however, that she has plans: Christmas is just days away and she has something that she needs to do: She wants to decorate the Christmas tree with her children. Frank, however, is unmoved: the matter is not up for debate. When Frank works late, Grace works late!

Is Frank, the big boss, human? Humbug!

Of course organizational narratives – even those that address persistent anxieties – do not need to be negative. Some bosses are fine specimens of humanity. And some, personally, uphold the rules of the organization as the following tale has been designed to demonstrate.

I was quaking I can tell you. Although, I'd been working as a plant security guard for some years I'd never actually encountered the big boss; you know the Head Honcho. I recognized him, of course, he features in the company's adverts for goodness sake. I mean when I'm in the City, he's there too on huge billboards, 40 foot tall.

Anyway I was on 'gate duty' when this big black car pulled up. I stopped the car – as I'm supposed to – and asked the driver and the rear-seat passenger for their security passes. The driver – it was Bob from the motor pool – hands his over nice as you like. He knows the score. But the big boss decides to play it differently. He's all, 'Don't you know who I am?'

Well I'm now shitting my pants. I say, about as calmly as I can,

'Well, sir, you certainly look like the Company Chief Executive, but I cannot be sure and my instructions are very clear. I cannot allow admittance to anyone who is not carrying ID.'

I expected that this would settle the matter, but he pipes up,

'But you do know who I am and I'm in a hurry. So be a good chap and raise the barrier.'

I say, 'I'm sorry, sir, that is simply not allowed. I must see your ID.'

And he replies, 'So, you're going to push it. You're telling me that you're not going to let me on to the site until I produce my ID.'

And I find myself saying, 'Yes sir that's about the size of it.'

I looked at him. And he looked at me – cold like; unsmiling. And then he reaches into his inside pocket and with a huge smile on his face he announces, 'Good man. I wish some of the Executive had your backbone', and hands me his ID.

I would say that I inspected his ID before handing it back, but that would be an exaggeration. I looked quickly at the photograph and handed it back to the boss; spluttered something about having a good day and then opened the barrier.

My knees were still shaking an hour letter when this big black car approaches the exit.

As the car approaches me, it slows down and the rear window lowers. I lean in to check the IDs and the big boss, addresses me by name, 'Mike,' how he knew my name I don't know, he says 'Do you like football?'

'Yes' I reply.

'Yes,' he says 'I heard as much inside. I'll have four tickets sent to you so that you can take your family to the game'.

These days the big boss always produces his card with a smile and a flourish ... and sometimes we chat about the match.

Gawd! They're having an awful season.

* * * *

Concluding comments

This, the opening chapter of our workbook, has been designed to allow you to reflect critically upon the nature of organizational culture. It has also been configured to allow you to understand the manner in which an appreciation of storytelling practices might enable purposeful cultural intervention within your organization.

Chapter 1 has offered:

• Critical reflections on 'culture', 'management' and 'storytelling' liberally illustrated by examples.

In particular, Chapter 1 has offered:

• A re-view of 'culture' designed to make space for ideas; for voices; for forms of expression generally written-out of 'popular management'.
• An analysis of 'sensegiving' and 'sensemaking' narratives.
• Illustrations of epic, comic, romantic and tragic story-forms.
• A review of 'elaborate', 'terse' and 'audience-centred' accounts of organizational storytelling.
• Reflections on the 6F factors often invoked in the name of narrative coherence.
• Critical reflections on the uniqueness paradox.

The discussion of this 'paradox' has been designed and located to remind us of the manner in which bottom-up tales challenge the understanding of 'culture' developed within 'popular management'. Furthermore, the analysis of the 'uniqueness paradox' developed in this chapter has been offered as a means of redeeming organizational storytelling; shifting this *from* a top-down project with imperial ambitions to become instead a means to reveal, to redeem, to comprehend the complex plurality of organizations so that a means may be found to work with rather than against the interests of those who, when all is said and done, actually deliver the organization's promises.

In Chapter 2 we will continue with our attempts to improve your story-telling practice as we reveal a number of maxims which, I suggest, you should bear in mind if you hope to use stories productively within organized settings.

Notes

1 This is meant as a humorous projection of course and yet the truth is (a) that catalogues for such luxury goods do exist and (b) that those who advertise their wares in these catalogues have done very well since the crash of 2008!
2 This latter suggestion is, it is worth noting, central to the rhetoric that shapes 'popular management'.
3 E.P. Thompson makes this distinction explicit as he introduces his, now classic, *The Making of the English Working Class*. Indeed he is careful to point out that when he speaks of England and the English working class he is *not* speaking of Britain. His study is, he tells us, of England and the distinctive experience of the English working class. This is refreshing at one level since England and Britain are often conflated in the minds of the English and in the minds of, for example, the Germans and the French. Yet Thompson undoes all this good work, in my mind, when he draws attention to the manner in which English history departs from the experience of its northern neighbours: 'The Scotch', he tells us, have their own history. This is accurate, of course, as is the fact that no Scot would ever (and I do mean ever) refer to 'the Scotch' or to 'Scotchmen'. If cultural analysis tells us anything it is that small things (such as this) make a big difference.
4 England's soldiers were encouraged to volunteer with their pals and were often formed into units with others drawn from their 'Shire' or, in larger conurbations, from their place of employment. This policy meant that in the aftermath of a large battle a small town or village might, in effect, lose an entire generation of its young men.
5 I chose to reproduce Sillitoe's reflections on this issue but in truth I am spoiled for choice and might have reproduced similar extracts from any number of authors including George Orwell (2000) and James Barke (1946) to name but two from many potential allies on this matter.
6 This is a common grammatical mistake: to speak of 'alternate facts' is to suggest that one should pay attention to every other 'fact' in a sequence!
7 I was inclined to believe that death comes to us all. Does the author know something that I don't?
8 The breadth of this estimate surely tells us rather a lot about the extent to which these lives were valued!
9 *Stans* – following the tragic case of a fan of the rapper Eminem – are, even by the standards of 'fan-boys', obsessive individuals who have an unhealthy interest in the artists that they admire.

References

Aristotle (1965) *The Politics*, trans. T.S. Dorsch, Penguin: London.
Barke, J. (1946) *The Wind that Shakes the Barley*, Collins: London and Glasgow.

Beigbeder, F. (2005) *Windows on the World*, Harper-Perennial: London.

Bendix, R. ([1956] 1963) *Work and Authority in Industry*, Wiley: New York.

Berendt, J. ([1994] 2009) *Midnight in the Garden of Good and Evil*, Sceptre: London.

Beynon, H. (1979) *Working for Ford*, Penguin: Harmondsworth.

Boje, D. (1991) 'The Storytelling Organization: A Study of Performance in an Office-Supply Firm', *Administrative Science Quarterly*, 36: 106–126.

Boje, D. (2001) *Narrative Methods for Organizational and Communication Research*, Sage: London.

Burrell, G. (1997) *Pandemonium*, Sage: London.

Chomsky, N. (2003) *Understanding Power: The Indispensable Chomsky*, Vintage: London.

Clark, T. and Greatbatch, D. (2002) 'Knowledge Legitimation and Affiliation Through Storytelling: The Example of Management Gurus', in Clark, T. and Fincham (eds), *Critical Consulting: New Perspectives on the Management Advice Industry*, Blackwell: Oxford.

Collins, D. (1998) *Organizational Change: Sociological Perspectives*, Routledge: London and New York.

Collins, D. (2000) *Management Fads and Buzzwords: Critical-Practical Perspectives*, Routledge: London and New York.

Collins, D. (2007) *Narrating the Management Guru: In Search of Tom Peters*, Taylor & Francis: London and New York.

Collins, D. (2013) 'In Search of Popular Management: Sensemaking, Sensegiving and Storytelling in the Excellence Project', *Culture and Organization*, 19(1): 42–61.

Collins, D. (2018) *Stories for Management Success: The Power of Talk in Organizations*, Taylor & Francis: Abingdon, Oxon and New York.

Collins, D. (2020) *Management Gurus: A Research Overview*, Taylor & Francis: Abingdon, Oxon and New York.

Collins, D. and Rainwater, K. (2005) 'Managing Change at Sears: A Sideways Look at a Celebrated Tale of Corporate Transformation', *Journal of Organizational Change Management*, 18(1): 16–30.

Deal, T.E. and Kennedy, A.A. (1982) *Corporate Cultures*, Penguin: Harmondsworth.

Denning, S. (2001) *The Springboard: How Storytelling Ignites Action in Knowledge-Era Organizations*, Routledge: London.

Edwards, P.K. (1986) *Conflict at Work*, Blackwell: Oxford.

Esler, G. (2012) *Lessons from the Top: How Successful Leaders Tell Stories to Get Ahead and Stay Ahead*, Profile Books: London.

Fayol, H. (1949) *General and Industrial Management*, Pitman: London.

Feldman, S.P. (1986) 'Management in Context: An Essay on the Relevance of Culture to the Understanding of Organizational Change', *Journal of Management Studies*, 23(6): 587–607.

Gabriel, Y. (2000) *Storytelling in Organizations: Facts, Fictions and Fantasies*, Oxford University Press: Oxford.

Gabriel, Y. (2004) 'Narratives, Stories and Texts', in Grant, D., Hardy, C., Oswick, C. and Putnam, L. (eds), *Discourse and Organization*, Sage: London.

Gioia, D.A. and Chittipeddi, K. (1991) 'Sensemaking and Sensegiving in Strategic Change Initiation', *Strategic Management Journal*, 12: 433–448.

Greatbatch, D. and Clark, T. (2005) *Management Speak: Why We Listen to What Management Gurus Tell Us*, Routledge: London.

Hofstede, G. (1980) *Cultures' Consequences: International Differences in Work-Related Values*, Sage: California.

82 *Organizational culture*

Krishan, P. (2019, 15 November) 'Racist Patients Could Be Compromising Their Own Care', *i*.

Kuper, A. (1993) *Anthropology and Anthropologists: The Modern British School*, Routledge: London.

Lammy, D. (2019, 3 November) 'How Britain Dishonoured its African First World War Dead', *Guardian*.

Martin, J. (1992) *Cultures in Organizations: Three Perspectives*, Oxford University Press: Oxford.

Martin, J., Feldman, M.S., Hatch, M.J. and Sitkin, S.B. (1983) 'The Uniqueness Paradox in Organizational Stories', *Administrative Science Quarterly*, 28: 438–453.

Miles, R. (1982) *Racism and Migrant Labour*, Routledge, Kegan and Paul: London.

Mintzberg, H. (1973) *The Nature of Managerial Work*, Harper & Row: New York.

Orwell, G. (2000) *George Orwell: Essays*, Penguin: London.

Parker, T. (1993) *May the Lord in His Mercy be Kind to Belfast*, Jonathan Cape: London.

Pascale, R.T. and Athos, A.G. ([1981] 1986) *The Art of Japanese Management*, Sidgwick and Jackson: London.

Peters, T. and Austin, N. (1985) *A Passion for Excellence: The Leadership Difference*, Fontana: London.

Peters, T. and Waterman, R. (1982) *In Search of Excellence*, Harper & Row: New York.

Proulx, A. (2006) *Close Range: Brokeback Mountain and Other Stories*, Harper-Perennial: London.

Sacco, J. (2003) *Palestine*, Jonathan Cape: London.

Satrapi, M. (2003) *Persepolis*, Vintage: London.

Schein, E. (1985) *Organizational Culture and Leadership*, Jossey-Bass: San Francisco.

Scott, J.C. (1987) *Weapons of the Weak: Everyday Forms of Peasant Resistance*, Yale University Press: New Haven.

Sellar, W.C. and Yeatman, R.J. [1930] (1938) *1066 And All That: A Memorable History of England, Comprising All the Parts You Can Remember, Including 103 Good Things, 5 Bad Kings and 2 Genuine Dates*, Methuen and Co: London.

Seth (2006) *Wimbledon Green: The Greatest Comic Book Collector in the World*, Jonathan Cape: London.

Sillitoe, A. (1979) *Raw Material*, W H Allen: London.

Spiegelman, A. (2003) *The Complete Maus*, Penguin Books: London.

Steinbeck, J. ([1937] 1974) *Of Mice and Men*, Pan Books: London.

Steinbeck, J. ([1942] 1983) *The Moon is Down*, Pan Books: London.

Taylor, A.J.P. (1979) *English History 1914–1945*, Penguin Books: London.

Thompson, E.P. ([1963] 1972) *The Making of the English Working Class*, Penguin: Harmondsworth.

Trumbo, D. ([1939] 1994) *Johnny Got His Gun*, Touchstone Books: London.

Weick, K. (1993) 'The Collapse of Sensemaking in Organizations: The Mann Gulch Disaster', *Administrative Science Quarterly*, 38: 628–652.

Weick, K. (1995) *Sensemaking in Organizations*, Sage: London.

Wright, S. (1994) *Anthropology of Organizations*, Routledge: London.

Wright-Mills, C. (1973) *The Sociological Imagination*, Penguin: Harmondsworth.

2 Talking the talk; walking the walk

Talking the talk

In Chapter 1, we offered reflections upon the nature of management and upon the dynamics of social organization. We observed that organizations are now, routinely, discussed in cultural terms. Yet we noted that these accounts of the patterns of thinking and action that constitute social organization tend to be rendered in ways that deny the biographies and indeed the agency of those present.

In an attempt to overcome the limiting appreciation of social life perpetuated by 'popular management' and by 'guru theory' (see Collins, 2020) we have offered a critical review of 'culture' *and* reflections on the nature and processes of organizational storytelling. We have argued that, at an analytical level, organizational storytelling is central to the understanding of managerial work. Furthermore, we have suggested that storytelling should be considered to be central to the practice of management because stories offer access to those organizational ideas and orientations that need to be understood if purposeful change is to be negotiated.

In this chapter we will offer a selection of maxims *and* a series of questions designed to inform this negotiation. As we shall see these maxims (and the accompanying examples chosen as illustrations) have been designed (a) to inform your appreciation of storytelling processes and (b) to underpin the narrative endeavours that you will essay in chapters 3 and 4.

You will observe, I hope, that I do not offer *axioms* for storytelling. My truths are straightforward. But I would not assume that these are self-evident. Indeed you will see that I am careful to develop, to explain and to illustrate the guidelines which I use to shape my own storytelling endeavours.

This story is about a time when:

The underlying theme of this tale is:
(Is this, for example, a tale about 'commitment', 'loyalty', 'loss', 'luck', 'insecurity', 'inequality' …?)

The person(s) reading/hearing this tale should feel:
(Is this a funny story? Will the audience feel pride, warmth, shame …?)

Hero/central character:

Assistants:

Predicament:

Agency:

Motive:

Credit:

Fixed qualities:

Notes for subsequent draft(s)
(This is where you reflect upon your next steps and what, now, needs to be done to improve the tale. Do you, for example, need to 'flesh out' the hero and his/her motivations? Does the predicament, perhaps, need fuller explanation/contextualization? Is your hero truly worthy of the emotional response you wish to solicit?)

Maxims for organizational storytelling

Maxim one: Stories constitute the organized world.

Maxim two: Stories have viral characteristics.

Maxim three: Stories are not reports.

Maxim four: Stories depend upon rapport.

Maxim five: Stories are local.

Maxim six: Stories contain 'unnecessary' elements.

Maxim seven: Stories improve with age.

Maxim eight: Stories belong to the audience.

Maxim nine: Stories have 'natural' narrators.

Maxim ten: Stories license conduct.

Maxim eleven: Stories require authenticity.

Maxim twelve: Stories test your conduct.

Maxim thirteen: Stories must not bore the audience.

Maxim fourteen: It is the person with the best, not the most, stories who will carry the day and define the future.

* * * *

Before we turn to a more detailed consideration of my storytelling maxims it may be worth taking a few moments to reflect upon the storytelling *pro forma*. On the page opposite you will find that I have developed and annotated a *pro forma*, designed to help you to structure tales in response to the challenges laid before you throughout the remainder of Chapter 2.

Please take a few moments to reflect upon this *pro forma*. Annotate it further if this helps!

Walking the walk

Maxim one: Stories constitute the organized world

Despite our everyday dismissal of 'anecdotal evidence' stories are not to be considered as subordinate to the other narratives (such as those that deal in 'facts', 'reports', 'samples' and 'statistical inference'). These scientific narratives do play an important function in our organizations, but when we seek to position stories as mere 'anecdotes' subordinate to *real* facts we overlook the extent to which what we do and who we are is constructed through the tales we tell ourselves.

Stories, as Weick (1995) makes plain, express who we are. Indeed they often provide the resources necessary to articulate what we *should* do under conditions of uncertainty and/or ambiguity.

Stories, meaningfully, communicate the possibilities that shape our present and future selves. And that is, I suppose, why we read fables and fairy-stories to our children.

If they are to grow into sensible adults our children need to understand the fate of 'the boy who cried wolf' and the larger lessons that may be gleaned from the study of Aesop's fables. Indeed a reading of 'The Pied Piper of Hamlin' very usefully communicates, to me, what happens when we seek to cheat others or to evade our obligations. What stories did you learn that set your moral compass?

What story would you tell your ten-year-old self?

What is your story now?

How will this story shape your future self?

And how might your story be applied to influence the sensemaking of your colleagues?

Take a few moments now to respond to these questions.

Maxim two: Stories have viral characteristics

Stories have a viral character and like the influenza virus (for example) depend upon hosts for their transmission. Stories survive, therefore – they are remembered and retold – only when they reflect the needs and orientations of the social group.

Stories that lack resonance within their host communities simply die from neglect. Put simply: Stories denied an agreeable host will not spread. They will be, in any sense, non-communicable!

* * * *

When my mother died just a few years ago I gathered with my own immediate family and with my brothers, sisters, nieces, nephews and cousins (etc.) to celebrate my mother's life. My mother had lived to a grand age (she was in her 91st year) and we had many tales to tell. Indeed I was delighted to learn that my older cousins (many now in their seventh and eighth decades) always regarded their aunt Chris as 'a kind woman'; as a warming presence in an adult world that was not always reliably compassionate towards children.

During this family gathering we also shared tales of my father and his life. My father, Tom Collins, who died nearly 30 years previously, was a small, but strong, man; a man who died early because he was – I tell myself – suited to the spring and summer of life and would not have taken at all well to a decline into infirmity.

Tom Collins lived in a world rich with stories. He valued and expressed through his tales and through his conduct, the simple pleasures in life; warm soup; a sunny morning on the Firth of Clyde; the company of his daughters and, especially, the company of his dog. As a young man he had interrupted his apprenticeship to join the Royal Air Force and served as 'Flight Engineer' aboard Q-Queenie, a Lancaster bomber of 514 Squadron.

As we shared stories of our parents my eldest sister, Christine (named for my mother and now dead too) remarked that despite being the youngest of the family and despite being 19 years her junior I seemed to know more stories of my father's early life than did she.

My dear sister found this puzzling and asked why this was so. My answer, of course, was couched in a story. I reminded my sister that I would often attach myself to my father's company when he stepped out to visit friends and family. And my sister agreed that this was indeed true. I observed that, unknowingly (for I was not a 'bookish' child) I had adopted the habit of the *Hobbit* when in adult company. My sister was puzzled, so I offered the following:

> I was small then (truthfully I'm still a wee guy) and I would sit quietly in the company of the adults when Father visited, for example, his brother Owen and his wife Mary.
>
> When the tea and coffee was served I would eat modestly from the biscuit plate and after a time the adults would simply lose any awareness of my presence. I had become a Hobbit: I was present but absent; seen but invisible.
>
> Since the adults were now in adult company, they chose to share stories and reminiscences in an unguarded manner. I listened then, and because the stories were good, I chose to remember what I had heard.
>
> Forty years on – like some long-dormant virus – I found myself (re) activated by the company of my close family and was able to spread what I knew; what I had learned.

As I reflect upon my parent and their legacy you may ponder:

Who will host your stories?

If you don't know; what steps will you take to seek out and to identify 'hosts'?

And as you search out you 'hosts' ask yourself: When did you last share a coffee or lunch with someone beyond your team or on a different hierarchical level?

Maxim three: Stories are not reports

Stories do not have to be narrowly truthful or somehow 'accurate' and verifiable to be valued. They cannot be patently false of course but they can 'embellish' actual events and, as we learned through our study of the 6F factors, they can edit scenes to secure a useful and/or pleasing effect. After all, myths and stories that deal with superheroes and the supernatural (for example) remain popular and powerful even in our thoroughly cynical, modern world!

How many tales do you tell that begin with the words: 'I don't know if this is true. Deep down I do hope that *this* is true of course. But really it doesn't matter. True or false it's all the same to me because this is a great tale …'?

Are there tales within your organizational experience that might, now, be edited, adapted and/or re-framed to increase their reach and appeal?

Could you, for example, re-cast a character within an existing tale to reach a new audience or to suggest a different outcome?

Could you, now, re-work a tale that you have told before to secure congruence with the requirements of the Bechdel-Wallace test?

Maxim four: Stories depend upon rapport

Stories are intimate products of experience and imagination. Furthermore the ideas and orientations which stories project will reveal, often, the character of the storyteller.

If you want your colleagues and/or clients to tell you tales that get beneath the surface of the organization you will need to be patient and you will need to take time to build a rapport.

When I work within organizations to harvest tales, to catalogue stories, to assess orientations and priorities, I generally set up a series of meetings. I schedule these meetings for at least an hour because experience has taught me that it might take 45 minutes before the person I am chatting with feels able to relay a tale of their organizational life. There are exceptions of course. Some of those I chat to have tales tumbling from their mouths the very moment that they sit down before me. But if you want to hear good stories – especially if you want to hear tales that have a romantic component – you will need to take time to establish trust and rapport.

Smile! Nod! Smile with your eyes! Laugh. Laugh some more … and when the person you are with feels that they may trust in you, the stories will come.

But ask yourself now:

How will you make time to hear and to tell stories?

What will you do to allow your colleagues to entrust you with the more intimate details of their lives and dreams?

Is there a place within or beyond the organization where you can actively – or, like my Hobbit self, quietly – become a host and connoisseur of your organization's storyworld?

Maxim five: Stories are local

Stories reflect local truths. This concern with local truths has a positive aspect: It allows particular groupings to carve and to project their identities. Stories, therefore, may be used to create local understandings; close(r) relationships; 'in' groupings. Yet in so doing stories define 'the other', either explicitly or through silence and/or omission. Indeed we should concede that stories may indulge prejudice and/or unwelcome stereotypes that act, for example, to deny women full organizational membership.

Is there a story known to you that captures elements of your organized existence that are simply opaque to 'outsiders'? If so, sketch it now!

Is there a systematic bias in your organization's storyworld? Is the Accounts Department, for example, always represented in a negative way?

Could you, now, craft a story to challenge 'othering' processes crystallized through and within your organization's storyworld?

Could you revisit a familiar organizational story, now, to 'spread the love' and to redistribute credit in a way that makes 'insiders' of those who are, presently, 'outsiders'?

Maxim six: Stories have 'unnecessary' elements

A few years ago when I was employed in a senior capacity at a university in England I was invited to attend a Senior Leadership Team 'development day' on storytelling. It is typical of modern British universities, I think, that they will pay (through the nose) for such events while ignoring or indeed devaluing the research undertaken by colleagues.

But I digress. And I am, of course, telling you something about my identity and my orientations as I do so …

To return to my point: during this 'development day' (hosted by a lovely bloke who wouldn't recognize the landscape of the debate on organizational storytelling if it bit him on the arse – *OK, I'll stop projecting now*) each of those present was required to tell a story. I promptly took my place (figuratively) at the back of the queue and sat, Hobbit-like, to listen to my colleagues.

Some of the tales were good; some were, frankly, disappointing. But the most disheartening part of this experience, for me, related to the fact that my colleagues often seemed to lose their nerve while they were speaking and would suddenly announce: '… well, to cut a long story short …' before proceeding to a hasty conclusion that robbed the tale of its energy and its moral.

It is true, of course, that when you tell a story you need to be careful to keep your audience engaged. When you sense you are 'losing the room', therefore, you may need to make adjustments to your tale. But you must not automatically assume that you should rush your tale to a conclusion. The audience will, I assure you, forgive you for a tale that, for a time, loses direction and/or energy, so long as the arc of your narrative delivers an outcome that is useful and pleasing. When you sense that you are 'losing the room', therefore, don't flee the stage. Instead you may choose to insert elements within your narrative that in other settings would be considered 'unnecessary'.

Charles Dickens ([1841] 1992) is, for me, the Master of Meanders. His texts, frankly, contain many textual elements that are 'unnecessary' and yet truly delightful.

As he sets the scene for his famous *Christmas Carol*, for example, Dickens tells us the following: 'Marley was dead: to begin with' (1).

And then, just a few moments later, he inserts the most wonderful textual 'meander'. In a 'report' the passage which I will reproduce below would be considered *prolix*; unwelcome; unproductive; unnecessarily wordy. Yet in the tale rendered by Dickens this 'meander' is not only welcome it is prized by all those who know and love the work:

> Old Marley was dead as a doornail. Mind! I don't mean to say that I know, of my own knowledge, what there is particularly dead about a doornail. I might have been inclined, myself, to regard a coffin-nail as the deadest piece of ironmongery in the trade. But the wisdom of our ancestors is in the simile; and my unhallowed hands shall not disturb it, or the Country's done for. You will therefore permit me to repeat, emphatically, that Marley was as dead as a doornail.
>
> (1–2)

The Scots (not Scotch!) comedian, Chic Murray, showed similar mastery of the meander as he performed his comic routines. Within a famous tale that required the narrator to present himself at the front door of an acquaintance, Chic offers the following aside: 'She opened the door in her night-dress … funny place to have a door'.

If you have the courage to announce a tale within an organized setting, be sure to take your courage in both hands. Don't rush the tale! Do not fail your audience!

Don't short-change the ending by galloping headlong through the middle parts of your narrative: Your tales need to work as narrative units and it is in 'the middle' that character traits and motivations are developed.

You may, of course, have briefer and more elaborate renderings of your favoured tales depending upon context. But you should not 'cut the story short' through timidity.

Whenever you announce a tale you form a compact, a covenant, with your audience: Your audience will happily trade their silence for entertainment and edification so long as you command their attention and generate a mutually pleasing outcome.

Meanders in your speech and text will be welcome and will be considered productive in this context where they add to the experience.

When did you announce a story and yet fail the tale?

What did you learn from this experience?

Given the opportunity again, to render this tale, what would you now do differently? Make a few notes now!

Is there 'a meander' that you might now develop and insert in a tale?

Maxim seven: Stories improve with age

Stories depend upon embellishment.

We understand intuitively that stories offer edited versions of experience. Indeed we are generally comfortable with the understanding that stories develop and improve as they are repeated and revised.

Take a story that you are familiar with ... how could you add to this tale to improve its reception?

Are there elements present that you might enhance or indeed exaggerate (perhaps for comic effect)?

Are there stories familiar to you that others would enjoy and repeat ... if only they were aware of them? When and how will you share these tales?

Is there an old story that might now be retold in a new way?

Make a few notes now!

Sketch a revised tale.

Maxim eight: Stories belong to the audience

Stories with hosts travel quickly. Yet as they travel, stories tend to mutate. This potential for mutation implies that storytellers, especially within an organizational context, may need to take steps to craft and to curate their preferred narrative understandings.

To tell a tale and to have this believed, enjoyed and repeated, you will need to add detail, texture and colour to your narrative. Add too much detail, however, and you risk converting your story into a report which will invite fact-checking on the part of the audience.

Each and every time you announce a story, therefore, you must recognize that in so doing you will need to tip-toe a route within and around narrative forms. Forrester (1956) captures the tensions associated with the narration of events and processes and in so doing offers, for me, a rather persuasive rationale for the exercise of 'poetic licence' and an acknowledgement that the consent of the audience needs to be won.

In the frontispiece for his biographical account of the life of R.S. Tuck (a British fighter pilot who was decorated for bravery during the Second World War), Forrester is careful to speak to those who, at some level, know his story through shared experience:

There are no fictitious characters in this book, but there are a few fictitious names. It seems to me that so long after the war it would be needlessly cruel to reawaken anguished memories for the families of those Royal Air Force men who did not die quickly or cleanly, or who died stupidly; those who contracted unpleasant diseases or suffered extreme hardship in Nazi prison camps or 'on the run'; the one or two who weakened and failed their comrades … So I have changed the names, but not the facts. The facts are part of the story.

(6, ellipses in original)

And yet 'facts' can overload a story and in so doing undermine your attempts at 'sensegiving'.

Greatbatch and Clark (2005) suggest that management gurus understand this tension rather well. They observe that in their seminar performances, gurus carefully frame their storytelling in order to forestall the interruptions of those who would, through a pointed interjection, seek to convert a 'story' into a 'report'. Thus Greatbatch and Clark suggest that management gurus avoid saying things like: 'Wang Laboratories had a structure that was quite unlike any other and acted to foster innovation …',[1] because they are aware that someone in the audience might respond: 'Well I worked 10 years for Wang and what you are suggesting is baloney …'.

Instead, the authors suggest that gurus will often choose to disguise the identity of the organizations they are discussing: 'A well known, and well-regarded, organization for which I provided consultancy services had a remarkable structure that …'.

Foxboro, a company discussed in *In Search of Excellence* (Peters and Waterman, 1982), demonstrates another means by which organizational storytelling may be safeguarded against unhelpful revision. In this instance, however, the protection is provided not by anonymity but by institutionalization.

As Peters and Waterman (1982) tell the tale, Foxboro was, in the late 1970s, a company in trouble. A 'high tech' company, Foxboro had bet its future on a key technological development but had been unable to bring this to market. In desperation, key personnel began to put in working days which stretched long into the night. Until one fateful evening when, just as all seemed lost, a key scientist managed to construct a working prototype of the long-sought-after innovation. Relieved and flushed with success, the scientist rushed from his laboratory in order to find another soul so that, together, they might share and give thanks for this breakthrough.

When I tell this tale I like to paint a (verbal) picture of the scientist, flushed with success, rushing from his lab along a dimly lit corridor, an unbuttoned lab coat flapping in his wake. Taking up the story, Peters and Waterman (1982) tell us that our flushed scientist made it to the company president's office where he outlined the features of the working prototype that would save the company.

Typically, I place the president in a large, comfortable and stylishly appointed office when I recount these events. I allow the scientist to barge in to the office (it seems sensible to assume that the assistant to the president left for home some hours ago and in any case allowing the scientist to enter unannounced adds to the drama). Furthermore I like to suggest that the office is in shadow save for the small pool of light produced by a desk lamp. *Can you, now, picture the scene?*

Commenting on the events that will unfold in this setting, Peters and Waterman (1982) tell us that the president found the scientist's prototype to be both useful and elegant. Perhaps unsurprisingly, therefore, the president felt that he should – there and then – produce some tangible means of recognizing the scientist's company-saving achievement. Indeed Peters and Waterman tells us that, during this interaction, the company president began rooting around in his desk drawers in an attempt to find a suitable token.

Taking up the tale again Peters and Waterman tell us that while rifling the contents of his desk drawers the president discovered a plump, yellow, banana; a leftover from lunch. Relieved, he snatched the banana from the drawer, thrust it into the hands of the, now, slightly bewildered scientist, and announced something along the lines of: 'Great job. You've saved the company. Have a banana.'

Discussing the significance of this tale, Peters and Waterman (1982) suggest that it has become a part of Foxboro's folklore. Furthermore, they suggest that the story has become institutionalized, and so, protected to some degree from revision because those who would make a contribution to the company have an exemplar to emulate and when they do so their endeavours are rewarded with a coveted 'golden banana' lapel pin.

Given the Foxboro experience it seems sensible to suggest that when you have found a story that produces useful managerial outcomes you should take steps to protect its core narrative. To this end you might find it useful to call to mind a story that you find productive and ask:

What steps might I take now to prevent my story being re-written in a non-productive manner?

If your company has an award what steps have you taken to craft stories around it? Indeed, you might ask yourself: What can I do to make the award and the tales which surround it special?

Finally you should ask: What might I do now to protect the prize (and the tale) from being devalued?

Maxim nine: Stories have 'natural' narrators

I was speaking to the board of a major bank recently. We were, of course, chatting about stories and storytelling. Indeed I was explaining to the assembled board members that research I had undertaken (in partnership with my colleague Dr Andy Taylor) on behalf of the bank had revealed a truly wonderful catalogue of genuinely good stories; the sort of stories that might be used, for example, at induction events to communicate something of the bank's ethos to new recruits.

During this discussion a tale (previously unknown to me) concerning the bank's CEO was shared.

It seems that early one winter morning a red-faced, heavily pregnant woman had entered a branch of the bank's premises in a highly agitated state. The woman's husband, who was also her business partner, had, it seems, died only recently. Now, on their own, these facts provide more than enough narrative resource for a promising tale, don't you agree?

Good! Now, hang on to that thought, because the story is about to get bigger and better!

The woman had entered the premises of – let's call it *Friendly Bank* – in a highly agitated state because her own bankers, let's call them *The Bank of Awful*, had been in touch to inform her that in the light of her husband's untimely passing they had no option but to call in her loan. The woman, who had only recently lost her husband and partner, was now in danger of losing her business and the home she shared with her now fatherless children. Nice, huh?

So the woman needed to know: Would *Friendly Bank* help? This heavily pregnant, highly agitated woman was given a large glass of water, a comfortable chair and some reassuring words by the manager of the branch. And some 40 minutes later she was back on the street with the understanding that the bank 'would look into the case' and 'would be in touch in due course'.

Now I don't know if the poor woman was reassured – I can't and won't put myself inside her head (not for this tale anyway) – but she returned home.

Two or three days later she was at her workplace, in the office she had until recently shared with her husband, when there was a knock on the door.

More bad news? *The Bank of Awful* come for payment-in-kind?

Nervously the woman levered herself from her chair and walked, with no small effort, to the door. Can you see her? Can you picture how she moves?

When she opened the door this heavily pregnant woman found, there on the threshold, the Chief Executive of *Friendly Bank* with a select delegation of his most senior and trusted specialists. 'We have come to help', he said.

And help they did ...

The business, which *The Bank of Awful* had been about to foreclose, was saved, thanks to the intervention of the Chief Executive of *Friendly Bank*. Indeed it flourishes still, as does its owner and her children.

This is, I think, a really great story and it is, I should add, typical of the organization, that I have named *Friendly Bank*, and (it needs to be said) its CEO. Yet this is a tale that works best when *not* rendered by the central character. This is a tale which works best as I have presented it, and as it was presented to me, in the absence of the boss.

Ask yourself: Are there tales that you now tell which might, more usefully, be entrusted to others?

Do you tell tales of your colleagues that acknowledge what they do well and/or when they have acted in character to do the right thing?

If so, when did you last share these tales?

Maxim ten: Stories license conduct

Storytelling has a capacity to shape thought and action within organized settings. It seems sensible to suggest therefore that in your attempts to shape and to co-ordinate the efforts of others you should take steps to ensure that the stories you produce actually promote the mode of thought and the forms of conduct that you believe to be necessary.

If you choose to tell a story which fails to communicate your core intentions you will license interactions and forms of conduct that may be contrary to your aims. Putting this more succinctly: If you want your colleagues to give great service do not indulge tales that mock or belittle your customers/clients!

So, as you announce a story, as you invite those around you to suspend the normal rules of conversational exchange, you may wish to pause for a moment so that you might first ask yourself:

Does my story reliably communicate the patterns of thought and action that I would like my friends, colleagues, stakeholders and/or co-workers to adopt? If your tales fail in this regard what will you do, now, to remedy this? Does your conduct model reliably the behaviour you would see in others?

Make a few notes now that will enable you to secure useful changes in your storyworld!

Maxim eleven: Stories require authenticity

Stories are, as we have established, 'world building' endeavours (Latour, 1987; Weick, 1995). In an organizational context stories construct and legitimate particular ways of thinking, feeling and acting. Stories, in short, cause and allow change.

Yet any change that you might seek to foster in future will build from what *is* now. So even as you attempt to reorient your colleagues, your employees and/or your customers through storytelling you must remain sensitive to the immanent quality of social organization. Moreover, you must remain sensitive to the dilemmas and tensions that structure daily life because it is these elements of our organized existence that will surely structure organizational storytelling (from the bottom-up).

Martin and her colleagues (Martin et al., 1983) capture this rather well. They observe that most organizations claim to be unique in cultural terms. Additionally, they observe that when organizational members are asked to account for these assertions of uniqueness they tend to warrant their claims through storytelling. Yet when these stories are compared across different organizations they are found to be remarkably similar.

Reflecting upon these storytelling practices Martin et al. (1983) suggest that seven key story-types tend to feature across a diverse range of organizations. Accounting for this finding, the authors suggest that these tales are constructed, and through repeated telling, are maintained within organizations because they reflect the persistent anxieties that are associated with the experience of working. Thus Martin et al. suggest that, otherwise, diverse organizations possess similar storyworlds because employees experience common anxieties in the face of power structures designed, variously, to control their interactions and to discipline their conduct.

In my own research (Collins, 2013) I have examined Tom Peters' storytelling in the light of the analysis developed by Martin et al. (1983). I suggest that there are clear differences between the storyworlds constructed by Peters and those documented by Martin and her colleagues: Tom Peters' storyworld seeks to narrate the organization from the 'top down' whereas Martin and her colleagues have explored the construction of social organization from the 'bottom up'. Furthermore, my research suggests that there is often a rupture between story-telling practices employed at the top of the organization and the stories that circulate towards the bottom of the organization. Indeed I argue that Peters' storyworld often lacks both authenticity and plausibility because it ignores a persistent and, increasingly, common anxiety in relation to *insecurity*.

So before you tell your colleagues; your employees; your suppliers or even your customers a tale, first ask yourself:

Is my story plausible?
Do the stories I tell reflect or acknowledge the persistent anxieties associated with working?
If your answer is 'no', what policy changes will you seek, now, to validate a new storyworld?

Make a few notes now that will enable purposeful change and development! Ask yourself:

Do my stories, for example, take account of the specific stressors that my demands for service, for commitment and for professionalism, more generally, place upon employees and/or colleagues?
Do my stories appreciate the problems and processes of work as these are experienced towards the bottom of the pyramid?

Maxim twelve: Stories test your conduct

You will forgive me I hope if I recount a tale that will be familiar to the readers of *Stories for Management Success*. You will forgive me, too, if I pause to make it plain that the tales rendered here are true. They are, I assure you, accurate renderings of events!

* * * *

Some years ago when I was a young and very junior member of the academic community I gratefully accepted a post at the University of Essex. Soon after I took up my employment the then Director of Research (who shall remain nameless) invited me to meet him in his office in order to discuss my research.

Prior to our scheduled meeting I was careful to prepare an engaging narra-tive around my research that might proclaim my awesomeness (I did warn you that I was a lot younger at the time!). Yet I need not have bothered. You see, despite the fact that the meeting had been scheduled to discuss *my* research, I never spoke more than two words during the whole encounter. *And it lasted fully 45 minutes.* I was, however, treated to an extended review of my Research Director's career, which demonstrated to his satisfaction at least that it was he who was awesome!

Before too long this Research Director was succeeded by another professorial colleague.

My new Research Director had, at that time, a mature, female, PhD student. This student placed considerable demands upon my colleague's time and since he guarded this jealously, she was deemed to be problematic.

The student in question, it seems, had recently taken to turning up at my colleague's office for impromptu and largely unproductive meetings. To forestall this unwelcome initiative my Research Director had developed an expedient and, initially, productive response: Whenever he heard this student approaching he would hide under his desk. On entering the office the troublesome student would find it unoccupied, would shrug her shoulders and, promptly, depart the scene. Or I should say that this is the situation that prevailed until one fateful day when, instead of shrugging and departing she decided to have a seat to await the return of her noble mentor. On that humid, midsummer afternoon my senior colleague was obliged to crouch, silently, beneath his desk for around 35 minutes until his troublesome student returned to her familiar pattern of behaviour and departed.

As I warm myself with these mischievous recollections you might, now, take a moment to ponder …While you are busy crafting tales of (your) epic endeavours what stories are your colleagues and co-workers telling of you?
Write a story about 'you at work': Are you a hero or a zero?
Now write a story about 'you at home': Are you a hero or a zero?

I guess that you are, like me, somewhere in-between. Given this, I suggest, that you may wish to think more carefully about how you cast your tales in future.
Ask:

Who are the heroes of my tales?
Do these heroes usefully reflect the demographics of my workforce?
Do these heroes reflect or usefully project my company's ethos?

Equally you should ask yourself:

What do the heroes of my tales, actually, say, think and do?
Are the heroes of my tales truly worthy?
Do my tales of organizational heroics usefully acknowledge plurality?
Do my heroes make sound ethical choices?

Finally you might ask yourself:

Do I personally model the conduct of the heroes represented in my tales?
When tested do I reflect the very best of the heroes represented in my narratives?

Maxim thirteen: Stories must not bore the audience

Epic story-forms dominate the tales that are published on the business of management. In these stories a handsome, dedicated, strong and gifted individual sets off, for example, on a quest to turn around a failing organization (see Collins and Rainwater, 2005) and, along the way, overcomes trials and ordeals that would break the spirit of a normal human.

I don't know about your preferences but I do not really enjoy these stories. Indeed I find them shrill.

I prefer stories that have both 'major' and 'minor' keys. I prefer tales which, metaphorically, play both the white keys and the black keys because I prefer to be entertained by those who understand that (whether life mirrors art or vice versa) experience is complex and nuanced.

I prefer my 'heroes' to have discernibly human qualities. Or, more plainly, I like my heroes to have flaws and imperfections. Indeed I will readily indulge sympathy for anti-heroes such as the central character of the recent film, *Joker*.

My thinking on this matter crystallized, I believe, when I read William Fotheringham's (2003) rather wonderful biography of the English cyclist, Tom Simpson, and Braddon's (1956) account of the life of Leonard Cheshire.

Simpson, the first British world champion of cycling and a credible contender for Tour de France victory, collapsed on the slopes of Mont Ventoux during a stage of the Tour and died soon afterwards. Some of those who have written about Simpson's life and death have sought to gloss over or have, indeed, sought to deny that he took performance-enhancing drugs. Fotheringham does not.

Fotheringham acknowledges that Simpson was, to put it coldly, cheating when he died. Indeed Fotheringham establishes that Simpson's heart failed, in part, because of the drugs he had taken to enhance his performance. Fotheringham therefore names Simpson as a cheat. Yet as he chronicles Simpson's life and career, he allows us to understand Simpson, the man, and the tragedy of his death. In so doing, Fotheringham offers redemption to his subject.

Braddon's (1956) very human biography of Leonard Cheshire has similar qualities. Leonard Cheshire was an RAF pilot during the Second World War. He flew more than 100 combat missions. He was decorated many times and was awarded the VC for his uncommon bravery. He was 'a hero'.

But Braddon's account of Cheshire is unlike many modern biographies and is quite unlike most modern managerial biographies because it makes it plain that Cheshire was an unlikely hero. Unlike so many cinematic representations of 'war heroes', for example, Cheshire was not apparently blessed with great physical or mental talents. He was a limited and unenthusiastic sportsman. He was also a diffident and at times delinquent student. Indeed, Cheshire was, by his own admission, a poor pilot who was (bizarrely) rather fearful of heights. Despite these aspects of his character, however, Cheshire led an elite squadron and pioneered, at great personal risk, a widely adopted system of precision bombing. Yet perhaps more importantly, Braddon makes it plain that in the post-war period Cheshire – the efficient warrior – selflessly devoted himself to the care of the elderly, the disabled and the infirm. Cheshire seems to me a man with properly human qualities; a man deserving of honour and respect. A flawed human but a rather perfect hero!

As you prepare your tales of organization you may wish to reflect upon the manner in which you characterize your heroes. Are these heroes one-dimensional? Do they exist within epics that are shrill? If you suspect that your characters are 'flat' and your narratives shrill you might now like to consider the merits of the comic form.

My disdain for the shrill epics of business endeavour and for the one-dimensional hero so often presented within managerial biographies may help to explain why I am naturally drawn to the comic story-form. That much is speculation of course. One thing is clear to me, however, that as a would-be storyteller you would do well to develop your comic capabilities because in my experience it is the comic story-form that finds hosts and, in so doing, circulates most readily and most freely in organized settings.

Comic tales travel freely and rapidly throughout organizational settings. Consequently comic stories are readily sustained in the organization's collective memory. Given this could you find some means of wrapping your message; your aspiration within a comic narrative?

Could you now develop a comic tale, say, to disarm your political opponents?

Could laughter be brought to bear on forms of action that you would oppose?

Take a few moments, now, to sketch in outline a tale that is both comic and productive.

Studying 'peasant politics', Scott (1987) suggests that laughter and mockery are weapons of the weak. We should add, however that these remain powerful weapons. As you construct your stories of change and worthwhile endeavour you should, I suggest, cultivate tales that laugh with others.

Those in positions of power who cannot laugh *with* may soon find themselves laughed at!

Take a few moments, now, to reflect upon your organization's sense of humour. Does your organization 'punch up' or 'punch down' when it constructs and shares humorous projections?

Maxim fourteen: It is the person with the best, not the most, stories who will carry the day and define the future

I lied! This is actually an axiom; a self-evident truth.

As an organizational storyteller your task is to find/craft those tales and tropes that connect with your audience. You do not need lots of stories but you do need tales that connect; tales that animate; tales that orientate.

In our next chapter you will have more opportunities to develop tales that will carry the day and define the future!

* * * *

Note

1 I have chosen Wang Laboratories in this illustration for two reasons. First, it featured in *In Search of Excellence*. Second, and more importantly, it is no longer trading.

References

Braddon, R. (1956) *Cheshire VC*, Companion Book Club: London.

Collins, D. (2013) 'In Search of Popular Management: Sensemaking, Sensegiving and Storytelling in the Excellence Project', *Culture and Organization*, 19(1): 42–61.

Collins, D. (2020) *Management Gurus: A Research Overview*, Taylor & Francis: Abingdon Oxon and New York.

Collins, D. and Rainwater, K. (2005) 'Managing Change at Sears: A Sideways Look at a Tale of Corporate Transformation', *Journal of Organizational Change Management*, 18 (1): 16–30.

Dickens, C. ([1841] 1992) *A Christmas Carol*, Cecil Palmer: London.

Forrester, L. (1956) *Fly for Your Life: The Story of Wing Commander Robert Stanford Tuck*, Panther: London.

Fotheringham, W. (2003) *Put Me Back On My Bike: In Search of Tom Simpson*, Yellow Jersey Press: London.

Greatbatch, D. and Clark, T. (2005) *Management Speak: Why We Listen to What the Gurus Tell Us*, Routledge: London.

Latour, B. (1987) *Science in Action*, Harvard University Press: Cambridge, MA.

Martin, J., Feldman, M.S., Hatch, M.J. and Sitkin, S.B. (1983) 'The Uniqueness Paradox in Organizational Storytelling', *Administrative Science Quarterly*, 28: 438–453.

Peters, T. and Waterman, R. (1982) *In Search of Excellence: Lessons from America's Best-Run Companies*, Harper & Row: New York.

Scott, J.C. (1987) *Weapons of the Weak: Everyday Forms of Peasant Resistance*, Yale University Press: New Haven.

Weick, K. (1995) *Sensemaking in Organizations*, Sage: London.

3 Storytelling exercises

Introduction

This chapter of the workbook has been designed to offer a range of writing exercises. These have been designed (a) to allow you to develop your skills as an organizational storyteller and (b) to encourage you to act strategically as you practise what is, after all, the primary means by which you can place yourself, your visions and your plans usefully in the company of others.

In this section you will find in excess of 20 exercises which will, variously, invite you to develop 'epic' and 'comic' tales. In addition you will find invitations to develop stories in response to specific phrases and/or opening statements.

But before we start a few remarks should prove helpful.

* * * *

Please don't assume that the tales you will produce in response to my invitations *need* to be autobiographical in nature.

Good storytellers, I accept, tend to base their narratives in personal experience but I don't think that you need to have faced the threat of summary dismissal to be able to craft a tale that will address, for example, the very reasonable concern that under some circumstances, your conduct or decision-making may have serious personal consequences.

* * * *

Please don't assume that you need to deal with the tasks in the order that I have arrayed them.

That said, *I do* advise that you might like to attempt the initial 'sketching exercises' I have developed before you move on to the storytelling exercises ... but the choice is yours. If you feel confident, just jump right in!

* * * *

This story is about a time when:

The underlying theme of this tale is:
(Is this, for example, a tale about 'commitment', 'loyalty', 'loss', 'luck', 'insecurity', 'inequality' ...?)

The person(s) reading/hearing this tale should feel:
(Is this a funny story? Will the audience feel pride, warmth, shame ...?)

Hero/central character:

Assistants:

Predicament:

Agency:

Motive:

Credit:

Fixed qualities:

Notes for subsequent draft(s)
(This is where you reflect upon your next steps and what, now, needs to be done to improve the tale. Do you, for example, need to 'flesh out' the hero and his/her motivations? Does the predicament, perhaps, need fuller explanation/contextualization? Is your hero truly worthy of the emotional response you wish to solicit?)

Please do commit your tales to paper. In other words, please write your stories down. That's why the *verso* pages are (nearly) blank!

And please don't think that your tales will be written just once. Stories improve through revision ... so long as you keep in mind (a) what it is you hope to achieve, (b) the nature of your intended audience and (c) their needs and orientations.

* * * *

On the page opposite you will find a *pro forma*. This *pro forma* has been designed to allow you to focus upon (a) the core processes of your story so that you can (b) decide the extent to which these processes reflect your desired outcomes. Indeed, you will see that I have annotated this *pro forma* in an attempt to guide you in its use.

You should, of course, feel free to annotate this further ... if that helps.

* * * *

Please don't be put off by the exercises.

My experience working with executives, for example, is that they will, despite their general action–orientation, manufacture just about any excuse to avoid actually getting down to the business of *writing a story*. Recognizing this, I have designed a number of character sketching exercises. These exercises take their inspiration from Taylor and Berkmann (1990) and have been designed (and positioned) to get you used to writing about your world; and about your colleagues in the absence of a plot device.

* * * *

Please don't feel that you must use the *pro forma* immediately.

Truthfully, I don't often use these at the outset. Indeed, it may be worth observing that I tend to use the *pro forma* when I embark upon the first re-draft of my storytelling. I employ the *pro forma* at this point for two reasons. First, I find that when I use the template at the outset my narratives become too mechanical. Second, using the template as a re-drafting tool, I find, usefully reveals the omissions – the gaps in understanding; in plotting; in 'motive' – that will need to be filled if my story is to become reliably persuasive of my core intentions.

* * * *

This Story Is About a Time When:

The Underlying Theme of This Tales Is:

The Person(s) Reading/ Hearing This Tale Should Feel:

Hero/central character:

Assistants:

Predicament:

Agency:

Motive:

Credit:

Fixed Qualities:

Notes for subsequent draft(s)

Please don't give up if you encounter difficulties initially.

If you find that when you turn to the challenge of actually writing a story you get a few lines down on to the paper and then 'dry up', don't fret. This is actually not at all unusual.

If you encounter some sort of block or feel hesitation in your writing, I suggest that you might turn to the *pro forma*. Fleshing out details on the core character and his/her motivation (for example) may overcome this temporary blockage *and* it will, at least, keep you writing!

My second suggestion to address 'a blockage' is, perhaps, less strategic but it is, I assure you, productive, if apparently paradoxical: When you encounter a block, when you don't know what to write next: Keep writing!

Neubauer (2006) advises that when you don't know what the next word of your story is (or needs to be) *just write* 'and'. And if this doesn't help immediately (and why would it) … *just write* 'and' once more … and if this doesn't help *just write* the word again, and again … and again. If you need to, fill the whole damn page with the word 'and'.

Trust me, before you reach the bottom of the page you will have something to write about … even if it's just how absurd some words become through repetition!

* * * *

Please don't edit your first draft.

Just write! You can (and will) rework your narrative when your first draft is complete.

* * * *

Please do have the courage to place yourself and 'your voice' in the text.

Don't worry too much about grammar. If necessary you can tidy that later and no one is grading your spelling. Your primary challenge at this stage is to communicate something meaningful to your audience: You dont need to spel wrds korectlee to comunikate an awthentik intenshun!

* * * *

Please don't remove your voice from the text: Readers/audiences value authenticity.

If you seek to efface yourself entirely you run the risk of sounding phoney!

* * * *

Please don't beat yourself up if you think your stories aren't good enough.

There's a word for this feeling: It's *horse-shit!*

OK, it's not a word that any self-respecting 'shrink' is going to use but it is nonetheless true: Your voice is authentically yours and is good enough.

Hey! You might want to inscribe that fact in your own hand-writing here on the page.

* * * *

Please do take risks with your stories.

In the context of this workbook what have you to lose? If the story you draft doesn't work ... change it in the next draft. Just, don't be timid!

* * * *

Please do choose to write about things that matter to you.

When your subjects matter to you they will come to matter to your audience. Indeed it might be helpful to note that, in Chapters 1 and 2 when I have written about my parents and family I did so with a lump in my throat. If you got any sense of my love for these people and the feelings of loss that I carry with me, still, then I will have done my job as a storyteller.

So ... allow yourself to communicate those things that genuinely matter to you.

* * * *

Please don't tell your reader things.

Show him/her instead the details that matter. You can, of course, tell us (for example) that your boss was red-faced with anger, but it will, I suggest, be more helpful to allow us to hear the tremor in her voice; the manner in which he turned his head to face you; the way her eyes turned from you to glance at the photograph of her kids; the sound of his nails drumming on the desk ...

* * * *

Please don't be bland.

You're not 'reporting facts', you're telling a tale. Entertain!

Entertain us with the details. And don't just tell us what can be seen ... you have other senses too. Engage these so that your audience will engage theirs!

And when you want to describe something as 'bland', don't use the term 'vanilla'. This is, now a cliché and it *is* empirically wrong: Vanilla is a wonderful flavouring. I can taste it now at that very point on my palate where its delicate flavour is released! Can you?

* * * *

Please do ... I was about to write 'have fun' because this is the advice that Neubauer (2006) offers, but this term doesn't quite capture what I'm after.

You see, I love writing. And I just love storytelling. Indeed all of my 'serious' academic work (even when I'm writing about financial regulation for example (see Collins et al., 2009; 2015)) is underpinned by a willingness to craft and to share stories.

Yet I don't always have 'fun' in the narrow sense that we generally use this term. I have 'fun' when I talk to my sons about films and football. I have 'fun' when my wife and I take our dog to the beach. Yet, when I wrote about the death of my sister (see Collins, 2007) I wasn't having 'fun'. In fact writing these words (within a larger account of the storytelling of Tom Peters – yes really!) pretty much turned me inside-out.

But I'm glad that I put my thoughts and my feelings about my sister (and my family) in print. What I put down on paper that day is personally meaningful and I'm told significant to those who (also) loved my sister.

So ... *please do* have fun ... but *please* also understand that you may tell stories that come from love ... even as you relate characters who carry envy, anger ... greed.

If we learned anything from the analysis of 'culture' and 'sensemaking' stories (in Chapter 1) it is surely that organizations are populated by individuals and groups that have passions and that these passions will find a means of expression, productively or otherwise.

Your job as a leader, your role as a storyteller, is, I suggest, (a) to notice these passions, (b) to take account of them and (c) to facilitate their legitimate expression, albeit in a fashion that takes account of goals that transcend the individual.

Are you ready?

Sketching exercises

The exercises developed below are based upon my experiences with executives in Britain and across Europe. The executives I have worked with understand, intuitively, the power of storytelling in an organized context and yet they often (initially at least) tend to resist my attempts to get them to write stories based upon their experiences.

I find this frustrating but I am not inclined to disparage my colleagues and clients. I am, however, keen to help you to overcome this natural reticence and have, therefore, developed a few writing exercise which I hope will help you. These exercises have been designed to start you writing and because they don't require a plotting device I find that they offer a bridge into a form of writing that, while it may not be new to you, is certainly quite unlike that routinely practised in the workplace.

Exercise one

When I work with graduate students I often confide that when I sit down to write, I enact a world wherein I assume that the very first person who will encounter my research dislikes me personally and will be keen, therefore, to fabricate some rationale to reject my writing.

When I make statements of this sort I am, of course, reminding my students that 'good' academic journals reject in excess of 90 per cent of the submissions they receive. And in this context I am trying to make my students aware that they will need to make a special effort (a) to explain their ideas so that they might (b) enrol an audience that is, frankly, wilful and often pretty obstinate (Latour, 1987).

I think that this is good advice, but if I'm honest my projection isn't quite true. When I sit down to write an article for a journal I don't actually have an image of the editor in mind. Instead I imagine my (first) reader as an intelligent lay-person; a smart non-specialist. My reader is, truthfully, my long-deceased father and his pals: Jimmy Craig; Sam Alexander; and George Skilling (to name but three).

These men, born in the 1920s and all dead now, were smart guys. Yet, by modern standards, they were lacking in education. My personal challenge, as I sit down to write, therefore, is to craft a narrative that renders, plainly and lucidly, complex ideas and concepts in a manner that would allow these individuals to grasp my argument and my convictions.

So … tell me about your 'natural audience'! Who do you really want to speak to when you announce a story?

You can name the person, if you like …

Of course, the 'person' you have in mind may be, as is mine, some amalgam of a few, key individuals. That's fine. At root I am interested in a 'sketch' that tells me something about how this 'person' (individual or collective) thinks, feels and acts.

And I'd like to know something of how this person (real or imagined) carries themselves and how they 'look'.

So close your eyes … take a moment …

Now prepare a word-sketch of the person that you hope will be moved by your storytelling.

Exercise two

Against my wishes my family acquired a puppy a couple of years ago. I was against this, not because I dislike dogs, but because I understood that the bulk of the day-to-day responsibility for the dog's care would fall to me. But my family is, apparently, a democracy and I was out-voted by my wife and two children. So it goes!

Nowadays I find myself rising especially early (even on the weekend) in order to walk the dog. Yet there are benefits to this activity beyond the companionship of a fine and clever creature.

Before we acquired our dog I knew few of my neighbours. Now I know many, although I should add that my neighbours generally greet my dog – by name – prior to acknowledging my presence.

For this task I'd like you to develop a 'character sketch' of your 'neighbour'. This might be someone you nod to on the train each day; or it might be someone that you work with and know fairly well.

To be honest it really doesn't matter … *Just sketch this individual!* What is the person you have in mind wearing now?

And what of their mannerisms?

Does the person, for example, tilt their head when they smile?

Does s/he snort when they laugh?

Does s/he have certain things that they (always) say/do?

Exercise three

In exercise two (above) you were asked to develop a sketch of a person's dress, mannerisms and movements (etc.). For this exercise I'd like you to construct a back-story for this person.

Here are a few prompts to get you started. You should of course feel free to add substitutes!

Think for a moment about your 'neighbour':

We know now how this person laughs, but who/ what makes them laugh?

If a stranger asked them for 'spare change', would they empty their pockets?

How did s/he get to be who they are?

If they are light on their feet (for example), do they owe this to dance classes in childhood?

Have they loved and been loved?

Have they dealt with disappointments in life? If so … how?

Exercise four

In this exercise I'd like to continue to stretch your developing narrative skills. For this exercise I'd like you to narrate a journey to work.

Please note: I'm not asking for an account of your journey (although I expect that you will root your narrative within an account of this experience). Nor do I want you to script a traffic report!

Of course I accept that whether your train arrives on time, or whether the road traffic is light on your journey, will have a material bearing on how the character you develop in your sketch will feel about their journey, but I don't want this to dominate the narrative. Instead I'd like you to write about what your character thinks, feels and dreams as they venture forth each day.

Here are a few prompts, just to get you started. You should of course feel free to make substitutions.

Think about the person making this journey:

Are they relaxed? Are they stressed?
Did they spill their coffee? Rip their newspaper?
Will they get a seat on the train?
Would they be aware, for example, of standing passengers on the train?
Would they offer their seat to another?

Exercise five

In this, our last 'sketching' exercise, I'd like you to turn the spotlight on yourself. This exercise is in two parts. In the first part I'd like you to write about yourself at your best.

What are 'the better angels of your nature' and how and when are these manifest?

In the second part I'd like you to talk about yourself when you are, let's say, less agreeable company. Mostly I'm a lovely bloke … but I can be impatient (with myself) and I'm pretty adept at what the British Police would call 'foul and abusive language'. Indeed I would add that I swear as only a Scotsman can, which is to say that, when aroused; when I catch my fingers in my desk drawer, for example, I am inclined to construct sentences wherein a single 'swear word' will appear first as noun, then as a verb before reappearing as an adjective coupled to a newly introduced 'swear word'. But enough about me!When you reveal yourself at your best, who are you? And what are you doing?
When you reveal yourself, let's say, at your worst, how is this manifest and who is the poor bastard who generally witnesses the spectacle?

Summary

The five 'sketching' tasks reproduced above have been developed as a form of 'warm-up' exercise to get you familiar with a form of writing, thinking and self-expression beyond that which (I assume) you normally encounter/develop within the world of work. I do hope you have found these useful!

Can I suggest that you might, now, like to spend some time developing and re-drafting these 'sketches' prior to attempting the storytelling exercises developed below?

Can I suggest, too, that when you have developed these 'character sketches' into a form that works for your purpose you might like to start the exercises all over again, perhaps, developing new descriptions and/ or new back-stories for the characters you have sketched?

Why am I seeking to engineer a pause, a delay?

The answer is straightforward really: Stories depend upon the interaction between a plot device and an agreeable (or disagreeable) character. The more time you spend writing and sketching characters, the greater will be your ability to develop useful vehicles for your stories; your concerns; your orientations. And this, after all, is why you picked up the workbook!

This story is about a time when:

The underlying theme of this tale is:
(Is this, for example, a tale about 'commitment', 'loyalty', 'loss', 'luck', 'insecurity', 'inequality' …?)

The person(s) reading/hearing this tale should feel:
(Is this a funny story? Will the audience feel pride, warmth, shame …?)

Hero/central character:

Assistants:

Predicament:

Agency:

Motive:

Credit:

Fixed qualities:

Notes for subsequent draft(s)

(This is where you reflect upon your next steps and what, now, needs to be done to improve the tale. Do you, for example, need to 'flesh out' the hero and his/her motivations? Does the predicament, perhaps, need fuller explanation/contextualization? Is your hero truly worthy of the emotional response you wish to solicit?)

Storytelling exercises

In this sub-section we will begin to draft stories, which is to say that I will now invite you to develop that special from of narrative which (a) places characters with hopes, fears, drives (etc.) within (b) a situation or predicament that will require (c) thought and/or action to (d) secure a resolution.

The first two exercises invite an autobiographical form of storytelling insofar as they ask you to develop/reflect upon a situation where *you* are central to the narrative. Later invitations, as you will see, are more open-ended. In subsequent exercises you may continue to write about your own experiences and you may continue to place yourself, directly, in the narrative … but you don't have to.

Indeed as our *maxims* (see Chapter 2) suggest, there may be circumstances where, to secure the desired effect, you may choose to efface your presence in the narrative.

Finally, you will observe that the invitations I have constructed begin and end with ellipses. This is a very deliberate and calculated choice: Our stories are always in the middle of something. When we announce the tale of *Cinderella*, for example, we step into the adult life of an unfortunate young woman. Yet this tale works only if we understand that throughout her childhood Cinderella enjoyed the love of her mother.

To acknowledge the fact that everything has a context; that our tales are but moments in a life and world that we share with others, our invitations begin (and end) elliptically …

This story is about a time when:

The underlying theme of this tale is:
(Is this, for example, a tale about 'commitment', 'loyalty', 'loss', 'luck', 'insecurity', 'inequality' …?)

The person(s) reading/hearing this tale should feel:
(Is this a funny story? Will the audience feel pride, warmth, shame …?)

Hero/central character:

Assistants:

Predicament:

Agency:

Motive:

Credit:

Fixed qualities:

Notes for subsequent draft(s)

(This is where you reflect upon your next steps and what, now, needs to be done to improve the tale. Do you, for example, need to 'flesh out' the hero and his/her motivations? Does the predicament, perhaps, need fuller explanation/contextualization? Is your hero truly worthy of the emotional response you wish to solicit?)

Exercise one

In this first storytelling exercise I'd like you to write a story about a time when you took charge of a situation.

You may have done so readily; you may have been reticent; you may have hesitated. Whatever you did ... I would like you to tell me how and why.

Please write a brief story that responds to the following

... *so I took charge of the situation* ...

This story is about a time when:

The underlying theme of this tale is:

The person(s) reading/hearing this tale should feel:

Hero/central character:

Assistants:

Predicament:

Agency:

Motive:

Credit:

Fixed Qualities:

Notes for subsequent draft(s)

Exercise two

In this situation I'd like you to reflect upon a moment in time when you acted as 'leader'. Please note I don't want you to write an essay on the academic models that contest the nature of leadership and its processes, although you may well choose to index these matters in your tale. Instead I'd like you to write a situation when you provided leadership.

What did you do?
How did you act?
What did you do to signal your leadership? Why did you do this? And was it productive?
And what have you learned?

Please write a brief story that responds to the following:
... we looked one to another and we all understood that it was time ...

This story is about a time when:

The underlying theme of this tale is:

The person(s) reading/hearing this tale should feel:

Hero/central character:

Assistants:

Predicament:

Agency:

Motive:

Credit:

Fixed Qualities:

Notes for subsequent draft(s)

Exercise three

Thanks to a certain Scottish poet (and an American novelist) I understand very well that the best laid plans (of mice and men) can often become derailed.

In this exercise I'd like you to develop a story about 'a screw up'. Your tale may be positive or negative, tragic or comic. All I ask is that you construct a narrative arc that addresses a situation (real, imagined or embellished) where a mistake impacts upon the lives and choices of characters in a dramatic situation.

Please develop a story that responds to the following:

... there was a screw-up ...

This story is about a time when:

The underlying theme of this tale is:

The person(s) reading/hearing this tale should feel:

Hero/central character:

Assistants:

Predicament:

Agency:

Motive:

Credit:

Fixed Qualities:

Notes for subsequent draft(s)

Exercise four

This exercise has some potential overlap with the exercise above insofar as both may index an account of 'a screw-up'. Indeed you might choose to consider this exercise as a continuation of the exercise above; a sequel if you will.

Alternatively you may choose to develop a counter-narrative; a reversal of the tale you developed in exercise three.

Whatever you choose to do please develop a tale that deals with:

    ... *getting away with it* ...

This story is about a time when:

The underlying theme of this tale is:

The person(s) reading/hearing this tale should feel:

Hero/central character:

Assistants:

Predicament:

Agency:

Motive:

Credit:

Fixed Qualities:

Notes for subsequent draft(s)

Exercise five

In this exercise I'd like you to develop a tale of the workplace that deals with 'luck'. Your tale may be 'tragic' insofar as it deals with 'bad' luck. Alternatively it may deal with 'good luck' and serendipity.

Of course you might choose to reject any notion of fortune and providence by offering a tale about 'making your own luck'. Indeed you may wish to discuss the 'dumb luck' that accrues to the undeserving fool. The choice is, of course, yours.

All I ask is that you develop a tale that deals with:

... *luck* ...

This story is about a time when:

The underlying theme of this tale is:

The person(s) reading/hearing this tale should feel:

Hero/central character:

Assistants:

Predicament:

Agency:

Motive:

Credit:

Fixed Qualities:

Notes for subsequent draft(s)

Exercise six

In this exercise I'd like you to develop a story about 'the first day at work'. This may be rendered in the first-person or in the third-person.

I have chosen this topic because the first day in a new job or in a new career represents a period of intense learning and risk. This 'first day' is a moment in your organized life when you are obliged to form new relationships and to navigate new power structures.

I took up my employment with the University of Essex on 1 August 1999. British universities often start new contracts on 1 August because it represents the start of a new financial year. This date is administratively convenient but it does not fully reflect the rhythms and dynamics of the university system. On 1 August most universities are, frankly, pretty empty places: The undergraduate students will have departed months ago and those faculty members not on vacation will be busy with their research. Consequently tumbleweed blows through the precincts of most British universities at this time of year.

I had expected that on 1 August 1999 I would find myself alone at my new place of work. I was wrong, however, because my new colleagues, Ian King and Robert Chia, had chosen to travel to work on that day; to greet me, to take me for lunch, and to show me around. Small things make a difference!

When I took up my post at the University of East Anglia in Easter 1997 the university was quiet and there was, as I recall, no welcoming committee. A few weeks later, however, on the first morning I was due to lecture to the undergraduate students, Ian Dewing (who had been on holiday when I arrived) knocked on my office door around ten minutes before my lecture was due to start: He had come to escort me to the venue!

What tale will you tell of the first day at work? Your tale may be one of stress and dislocation or it may be a tale of excitement and wonder. The choice is yours.

All I ask is that you develop a tale that takes the first day in a new organization as its focal point and uses this to create a meaningful account of what it so often means to be 'a newbie'.

Whatever you choose to do please develop a tale that responds to the following:

... it was the first morning in a new organization and ...

This story is about a time when:

The underlying theme of this tale is:

The person(s) reading/hearing this tale should feel:

Hero/central character:

Assistants:

Predicament:

Agency:

Motive:

Credit:

Fixed Qualities:

Notes for subsequent draft(s)

Exercise seven

In this exercise I'd like a story about *your* best day at work.

This tale could be based in experience or could be rooted in a fantasy. It may be narrowly related to the workplace or it might acknowledge the manner in which work intrudes into other spheres. Your 'best day' might be, for example, the day you met your partner or forged a life-long friendship. Indeed the story might be bittersweet. For example, two days after my sister Joan died I was due to lecture at the University of Essex. I drove to at work as usual, early that morning, but will confess that my heart wasn't really in it.

When I arrived at work my colleague, Ceri Watkins, was waiting. Ceri was not due to be in his office that day but, having heard of my news had made a special effort to get to work before I arrived. Ceri, I now understand, wanted to look me in the eyes. He needed me to know that he cared. And he simply had to be sure that I would be alright.

I don't think that this can count, truly, as my 'best day at work' ... but it is, despite the circumstances, a special memory.

However you choose to frame it, please develop a tale that addresses:

... my best day at work ...

This story is about a time when:

The underlying theme of this tale is:

The person(s) reading/hearing this tale should feel:

Hero/central character:

Assistants:

Predicament:

Agency:

Motive:

Credit:

Fixed Qualities:

Notes for subsequent draft(s)

Exercise eight

In this exercise I'd like you to develop a story about *your* worst day at work or, more specifically, the day after your very worst day at work.

This tale may be rooted directly in experience or it may be fantastical.

The tale may focus narrowly on the workplace or it may demonstrate an overlap between your work-life and your home-life. The choice is yours, all I require is that you develop a tale that takes as it central dramatic component the aftermath of a very bad day.

… on the day after what I now regard as my worst day at work …

This story is about a time when:

The underlying theme of this tale is:

The person(s) reading/hearing this tale should feel:

Hero/central character:

Assistants:

Predicament:

Agency:

Motive:

Credit:

Fixed Qualities:

Notes for subsequent draft(s)

Exercise nine

In this exercise I'd like you to develop a story that deals with 'wellness'. Many people, often quietly and painfully, struggle with mental health issues. Many of us, frankly, feel overwhelmed by the stress and anxiety associated with working.

In this exercise I'd like you to develop a tale that addresses the issue of 'wellness'. This tale may be rooted directly in your own experience or may be derived from another inspiration. All I ask is that you develop a tale that acknowledges and/or explores the manner in which issues associated with health and well-being feature in the life of your organization.

If a colleague was feeling anxious are you confident (a) that they would feel that they could talk to you and are you (b) comfortable that you would handle the conversation appropriately?

Or are you one of those monsters (and, yes, I know I'm projecting again) who believe that 'stress' is an invented ailment suffered by 'snowflakes'?

All that is required is that you develop a tale in response to the following:

… it seems to me that nowadays everyone's stressed and anxious …

This story is about a time when:

The underlying theme of this tale is:

The person(s) reading/hearing this tale should feel:

Hero/central character:

Assistants:

Predicament:

Agency:

Motive:

Credit:

Fixed Qualities:

Notes for subsequent draft(s)

Exercise ten

In this exercise I'd like to touch upon the issue of work–life balance. Many of the epic tales of organizational endeavour developed during the 1980s offered studies of 'commitment' which were pretty much total, and so, left, it seems to me, no legitimate space for the consideration of 'stress' and the need for 'work–life balance'.

In this tale I would like you to reflect upon this issue. To what extent do you and your employing organization grasp the concept of work–life balance in a meaningful sense?

You may have a good news story here ... you may have a darker tale to tell. All I ask is that you make the issue of 'work–life balance' a central component of your tale.

... *it is you see a question of commitment* ...

This story is about a time when:

The underlying theme of this tale is:

The person(s) reading/hearing this tale should feel:

Hero/central character:

Assistants:

Predicament:

Agency:

Motive:

Credit:

Fixed Qualities:

Notes for subsequent draft(s)

Exercise eleven

In this exercise I would like you to reflect upon the challenge of 'digital' business.

A revolution in digital technologies has made new products and indeed new modes of business available. Many organizations have detailed 'digital' strategies. But do they have, within this, 'people' strategies?

In this exercise I would like you to develop a story that addresses the challenge of digital through the eyes of a colleague or client whom you anticipate will be adversely affected. How do they understand the world? Are their concerns legitimate?

... digital isn't coming ... it's here and I'm worried ...

This story is about a time when:

The underlying theme of this tale is:

The person(s) reading/hearing this tale should feel:

Hero/central character:

Assistants:

Predicament:

Agency:

Motive:

Credit:

Fixed Qualities:

Notes for subsequent draft(s)

Exercise twelve

So far I have, while directing your actions to some degree, offered you considerable discretion in your storytelling. In this exercise, and in the three exercises that follow, I will constrain your choice somewhat insofar as I will invite you to develop particular story-types.

In this exercise I would like you to develop an epic tale.

Epic tales, as we noted in Chapter 1, deal with stories of triumph and endeavour. The characters in these tales are often pretty one-dimensional (handsome princes; noble peasants; charismatic CEOs; brave soldiers, etc.) because the 'epic' form tends to deal with journeys (real or figurative), obstacles and successes so that the reader/ audience present feels admiration for the hero.

For this exercise I'd like you to develop a tale of work and working that is 'epic'.

And can I remind you please that the hero does not need to be male … and need not be one-dimensional?!

This story is about a time when:

The underlying theme of this tale is:

The person(s) reading/hearing this tale should feel:

Hero/central character:

Assistants:

Predicament:

Agency:

Motive:

Credit:

Fixed Qualities:

Notes for subsequent draft(s)

Exercise thirteen

In this exercise I'd like you to develop a 'tragic' tale. Tragic tales are, of course, those narratives that visit some sort of disappointing outcome or reversal on the hero.

I'll leave it to you to decide whether this downturn in the hero's fortunes/prospects is minor or major, personal or professional.

All I require is that you develop a narrative arc, rooted in an account of work and working that allows us to understand why it is that the hero of your tale is suffering as the tale concludes.

This story is about a time when:

The underlying theme of this tale is:

The person(s) reading/hearing this tale should feel:

Hero/central character:

Assistants:

Predicament:

Agency:

Motive:

Credit:

Fixed Qualities:

Notes for subsequent draft(s)

Exercise fourteen

In this exercise I would like you to develop a 'romantic' tale. Romantic tales, it is worth observing, do not often feature in organizational storyworlds. Noting this absence, Gabriel (2000) suggests that:

a   People do not often develop romantic tales of the workplace because cultural norms (and indeed the writings of 'popular management') tend to portray such emotions as being inappropriate in the context of serious business matters.

b   Researchers seldom secure access to the romantic tales that circulate within organizations because they fail to develop the rapport necessary to allow their colleagues to feel confident in rendering that which is, so often, deemed to be contrary to the real business of management.

In this exercise I'd like you – boldly and proudly – to make a space for matters of love and romance. So, please, develop for me (and for yourself) a tale that deals with affairs of the heart in the context of the workplace.

Is it a love that's meant to be?

A love against the odds; a love forbidden?

The choice is yours.

This story is about a time when:

The underlying theme of this tale is:

The person(s) reading/hearing this tale should feel:

Hero/central character:

Assistants:

Predicament:

Agency:

Motive:

Credit:

Fixed Qualities:

Notes for subsequent draft(s)

Exercise fifteen

This exercise offers an invitation to develop a story-type that circulates widely and I should say rapidly within organized contexts. Here I'd like you to develop a comic tale.

Comic tales are, technically, the opposite of 'tragic' tales. Where tragic tales deal with a decline in fortunes, comic tales are, technically, those that conclude with an improvement in the hero's situation/prospects.

My invitation to you, here, is a little more constrained: I'd like you to make me laugh! Your humour may be physical – there after all fewer sights more funny than your best friend tripping over a kerb – or it may be more situational. However you choose to frame your humour, your challenge is straightforward: Please develop a tale designed to make your audience laugh!

This story is about a time when:

The underlying theme of this tale is:

The person(s) reading/hearing this tale should feel:

Hero/central character:

Assistants:

Predicament:

Agency:

Motive:

Credit:

Fixed Qualities:

Notes for subsequent draft(s)

Exercise sixteen

Towards the end of Chapter 1, we observed that many of the tales which circulate in organizations arise and persist because they relate to anxieties associated with work and with, for example, the insecurities and inequalities that arise in this context. In this exercise and in the six exercises that follow we will address these concerns concretely and directly.

We do this because if you are to intervene purposefully in the storyworld of your organization; if you are to place yourself usefully in the company of your colleagues you must be able to index their concerns. If your tales do not index the problems and anxieties that persist in organized contexts your narrative, and indeed your identity, will be rejected as bogus; inauthentic.

Please develop a tale that responds to the following:

… she had always wondered if people really stuck to the rules, and now she was about to find out …

This story is about a time when:

The underlying theme of this tale is:

The person(s) reading/hearing this tale should feel:

Hero/central character:

Assistants:

Predicament:

Agency:

Motive:

Credit:

Fixed Qualities:

Notes for subsequent draft(s)

Exercise seventeen

'Management', within textbooks developed for students, often appears as a logic; as a disembodied entity. Yet 'managing' is an activity carried out by people and enacted through people.

Your task in this exercise is to address this simple, often overlooked, fact. Whether or not you choose to redeem the character at the centre of the drama is, of course, down to you.

Please develop a tale in response to the following:

... so you're really asking is the boss actually human ...

This story is about a time when:

The underlying theme of this tale is:

The person(s) reading/hearing this tale should feel:

Hero/central character:

Assistants:

Predicament:

Agency:

Motive:

Credit:

Fixed Qualities:

Notes for subsequent draft(s)

Exercise eighteen

Have you ever sought promotion and failed to secure your goal? Have you ever watched a colleague 'in full flow' and thought to yourself, 'She is an inspiration'?

Or, less positively, have you ever looked at a member of your team and asked yourself, 'Who promoted that fool?'

If so this may be the storytelling challenge you've been waiting for! Please develop a story in response to the following:

… welcome to the organization. Pretty soon you'll start to wonder what it takes to get ahead here, so we'd better get a few things straight …

This story is about a time when:

The underlying theme of this tale is:

The person(s) reading/hearing this tale should feel:

Hero/central character:

Assistants:

Predicament:

Agency:

Motive:

Credit:

Fixed Qualities:

Notes for subsequent draft(s)

Exercise nineteen

This exercise is an invitation to develop a tale about dismissal. You may choose to make this an autobiographical tale or you may position yourself as the all-knowing narrator.

Equally this may be a comic tale, a tragic tale, an epic tale, or indeed a romance. The choice is yours. All I ask is that the prospect of dismissal is central to the plot and to the motivations of the hero.

Please develop a tale that responds to the following:

... *the question often arises 'will this get me fired?'* ...

This story is about a time when:

The underlying theme of this tale is:

The person(s) reading/hearing this tale should feel:

Hero/central character:

Assistants:

Predicament:

Agency:

Motive:

Credit:

Fixed Qualities:

Notes for subsequent draft(s)

Exercise twenty

This exercise invites you to reflect upon the manner in which working lives act to shape how we live and indeed where we live. Many of us work far from home because we do not want to visit undue disruption on the lives of our partners, children and – let's be honest – our pets (or maybe that's just me).

In this exercise I'd like you to develop a tale which deals with questions around relocation. This could be a 'good news' tale or a 'bad news' story, the choice is yours.

All I ask is that you make 'relocation' and the question as to the extent to which the employer will assist in this predicament central to your narrative.

Please develop a story in response to the following:

... so we may need to relocate ...

This story is about a time when:

The underlying theme of this tale is:

The person(s) reading/hearing this tale should feel:

Hero/central character:

Assistants:

Predicament:

Agency:

Motive:

Credit:

Fixed Qualities:

Notes for subsequent draft(s)

Exercise twenty-one

Most of us will make mistakes on a day-to-day basis. Some of these are relatively minor – forgetting keys; failing to charge your telephone – whereas others are altogether more serious – pissing off a key client; filling the car with petrol instead of diesel fuel ...

In this exercise I'd like you to develop a story, which deals with a mistake and the hero's fears regarding the consequences of this failure. Your tale may end well or badly. The choice is yours.

Please develop a story in response to the following:

... so now another choice had to be made: own up and face the consequences or ...

This story is about a time when:

The underlying theme of this tale is:

The person(s) reading/hearing this tale should feel:

Hero/central character:

Assistants:

Predicament:

Agency:

Motive:

Credit:

Fixed Qualities:

Notes for subsequent draft(s)

Exercise twenty-two

This exercise invites you to craft a tale that deals with the manner in which the organization deals with problems and obstacles.

Does the organization address problems or does it attack people?

Is the organization creative?

Is it ethical?

Will the hero 'fix' the problem and if s/he does so, do they behave well? Alternatively, does your hero simply benefit from the intervention of another or, indeed, from simple dumb luck?

The choice is yours! All I ask is that you develop a narrative wherein the central character becomes, somehow, implicated in a situation wherein a blockage needs to be addressed.

Please develop a story in response to the following:

... it was clear that something needed to be done ...

This story is about a time when:

The underlying theme of this tale is:

The person(s) reading/hearing this tale should feel:

Hero/central character:

Assistants:

Predicament:

Agency:

Motive:

Credit:

Fixed Qualities:

Notes for subsequent draft(s)

Exercise twenty-three

In this exercise, and in the exercises developed below, I will once again intervene to limit your scope for action because I want to offer you an opportunity to develop some more complex tales of organization.

I do accept of course that in your endeavours so far you may have, deliberately or otherwise, developed stories that mix and combine the story-forms that in earlier exercises we sought to separate. If you have, for example, already developed epic tales with comic undercurrents or tragic tales with a romantic element, I say well done: You're obviously a natural. If you have not done this, don't worry now's your chance.

For this exercise I would like you to develop an epic tale that contains comic elements. You may secure this, for example, through the development of a comical assistant. Alternatively you may engineer a comic scene or moment within the quest. Obviously the choice is yours.

All I ask is that you develop a tale that deliberately mixes and combines those elements that we have – for the purposes of analytical clarity – tended to separate.

This story is about a time when:

The underlying theme of this tale is:

The person(s) reading/hearing this tale should feel:

Hero/central character:

Assistants:

Predicament:

Agency:

Motive:

Credit:

Fixed Qualities:

Notes for subsequent draft(s)

Exercise twenty-four

In this exercise I am again inviting you to develop a more complex account of organizational life secured through the combination of the 'epic' and 'romantic' form.

You may secure this by focusing upon events within the workplace. Alternatively you may choose to extend your organizational tale beyond the confines of the office, warehouse or factory (to offer but three examples).

Your epic journey may be physical or figurative. Your romance may be *schmaltzy* or it may be more challenging.

All I ask is that you develop a tale that reflects the complexity of social organization *and* the lives of those who, for a whole variety of reasons, fall in love with unsuitable people, out of love with suitable people, or who yearn for someone who can never be reached.

Oh … and please don't feel constrained to develop a 'conventional' heterosexual relationship!

Your challenge is to develop a tale which usefully combines 'epic' and 'romantic' tropes.

This story is about a time when:

The underlying theme of this tale is:

The person(s) reading/hearing this tale should feel:

Hero/central character:

Assistants:

Predicament:

Agency:

Motive:

Credit:

Fixed Qualities:

Notes for subsequent draft(s)

Exercise twenty-five

In this exercise I would like you to develop a tale that combines the 'tragic' and 'comic' forms. This could, of course, involve laughter in the face of loss as so often happens when friends and family members gather for a funeral.

Equally you may use humour to leaven a tale that in other circumstances would be just too alarming. You may remember for example the exchange that occurs just moments after the first aeroplane hits the north tower in Beigbeder's (2005) novel?

The choice is, and stop me if you've heard this before, yours!

All is require is that you develop a tale that artfully combines the 'tragic' and 'comic' forms to develop a productive narrative that will usefully persuade your intended audience that your tale is sufficient to merit further reflection and indeed repetition.

This story is about a time when:

The underlying theme of this tale is:

The person(s) reading/hearing this tale should feel:

Hero/central character:

Assistants:

Predicament:

Agency:

Motive:

Credit:

Fixed Qualities:

Notes for subsequent draft(s)

Exercise twenty-six

Poetic stories contain elements – sights, sounds, metaphors, allusions and asides (to name but a few components) that would be considered unproductive and which would be, consequently, unwelcome in other narratives (such as reports). In this our final exercise I would like you to develop narratives that contain 'meanders'.

For this exercise you may wish to revisit one of the tales developed in an earlier exercise to develop a fuller narrative that, because it includes those elements deemed to be both unproductive and unnecessary in other narrative forms, will enable you to construct a tale that is more likely to become memorable and so portable.

Frankly I don't mind what you do … all I need you to do is to work creatively; to use language; word-play; emotional calls; vivid description (etc.) to engineer ' a meander' and in so doing to develop an account of the world that is engaging, pleasing, somewhat surprising, and so, worthy of repetition.

This story is about a time when:

The underlying theme of this tale is:

The person(s) reading/hearing this tale should feel:

Hero/central character:

Assistants:

Predicament:

Agency:

Motive:

Credit:

Fixed Qualities:

Notes for subsequent draft(s)

Concluding comments

The exercises developed in this chapter of the workbook have been designed as opportunities for you to challenge yourself as a writer and storyteller. They have been constructed to enable you to develop stories that will (re)connect with your intended audience(s).

To facilitate your storytelling endeavours I have developed five sketching exercises. These have been designed (and positioned) to encourage you to develop the style of writing that will create/capture those around you as characters with drives, emotions, needs and failings.

I suggest that you should return frequently to these exercises: Organizational stories are typically character-driven dramas. The success of your storytelling will depend therefore upon your ability to generate agreeably authentic characters for your dramas.

When you feel that you have exhausted these sketching exercises … you haven't! To refresh and renew the exercises all you need do is reverse the instructions.

I have in addition developed more than 20 storytelling exercises. You may have chosen to tackle these in the manner I have arranged them or you may have adopted a random approach. That's fine!

If you have tackled the exercises as I have arranged these you will have produced autobiographical tales before moving on to develop third-person narratives of the workplace. These exercises it is worth noting offer considerable choice over form.

The next exercises in the sequence I have developed constrain your storytelling somewhat insofar as they have instructed you to develop, in turn, 'epic', 'comic', 'tragic' and 'romantic' tales. Following Collins and Rainwater (2005) you may now wish to subvert these tasks. You could for example, now, attempt to convert the 'epic' tale you crafted to a 'comic' form!

Exercises 16–22 seek a connection with the work of Martin et al. (1983). These exercises, as you will recall, invited you to develop stories which reflect the persistent anxieties that arise in the context of the workplace. I suggest that you should pay special attention to these tales because these are the stories that circulate beyond the earshot of the elite that controls the organization.

The final exercises developed for you deal with what I have called 'meanders' and 'complex' tales. These exercises are rooted in an understanding that when you announce a tale you must be prepared to take steps to manage your audience and to secure its continuing enrolment (Collins, 2020). Storytellers who fail to appreciate this requirement will find that their ideas, orientations, dreams (etc.) are simply rejected by those whom they hoped to animate and to orientate.

The exercises dealing with 'complex' tales and textual 'meanders' recognize the wilfulness of audiences and their obstinacy before your plans/visions and have been designed, therefore, to encourage you to seek out and to place within your narratives those moments and movements that people find pleasing, and so, worthy of repetition. Good storytellers, I suggest, understand the power of such meanders and deploy these, artfully, to seduce and to beguile those whom they would enrol in their projects.

References

Beigbeder, F. (2005) *Windows on the World*, Harper-Perennial: London.

Collins, D. (2007) *Narrating the Management Guru: In Search of Tom Peters*, Routledge: Abingdon, Oxon and New York.

Collins, D. (2020) *Management Gurus: A Research Overview*, Routledge: Abingdon, Oxon and New York.

Collins, D. and Rainwater, K. (2005) 'Managing Change at Sears: A Sideways Look at a Celebrated Tale of Corporate Transformation', *Journal of Organizational Change Management*, 18(1): 16–30.

Collins, D., Dewing, I. and Russell, P. (2009) 'Postcards from the Front: Changing Narratives in UK Financial Services', *Critical Perspectives on Accounting*, 20(8): 884–895.

Collins, D., Dewing, I. and Russell, P. (2015) 'Between Maxwell and Micawber: Plotting the Failure of the Equitable Life', *Accounting and Business Research*, 45(6–7): 715–737.

Gabriel, Y. (2000) *Storytelling in Organizations: Facts, Fictions and Fantasies*, Sage: London.

Latour, B. (1987) *Science in Action*, Harvard University Press: Cambridge, MA.

Martin, J., Feldman, M.S., Hatch, M.J. and Sitkin, S.B. (1983) 'The Uniqueness Paradox in Organizational Stories', *Administrative Science Quarterly*, 28: 438–453.

Neubauer, B. (2006) *The Write-Brain Workbook*, Writer's Digest Books: Cincinnati.

Taylor, D.J. and Berkmann, M. (1990) *Other People: Portraits from the Nineties*, Bloomsbury: London.

4   Exploring the storyworld

Introduction

In Chapter 1, we offered a critical analysis of organizational culture. We argued that the accounts of culture that have been developed in and through 'popular management' are flawed analytically and limited practically because they offer accounts of what people say, think and do (at work) that have been ripped from context.

In an attempt to develop an appreciation of culture which builds from an understanding of *how* people talk, *what* people think and *why* they act in particular ways we have offered a critical account of organizational storytelling. Noting that the analysis of organizational culture is typically rooted in top-down, sensegiving accounts of storytelling, we have offered an analysis of sensemaking narratives. These narratives, as we have seen, are important because they have a capacity to reveal and to articulate the persistent anxieties that shape the experience of work from the bottom-up.

In Chapter 2 we outlined 14 maxims designed to prime you, the user of this workbook, for the complex challenges that arise when you seek to render the experience of social organization in and through storytelling. In Chapter 3 we developed a range of character-sketching challenges. In addition we produced more than 20 storytelling exercises, designed to allow you to refine your capability as an organizational storyteller. In this, the final chapter of the workbook, I will invite you to undertake a little research. In this section I will invite you to reflect upon the tales commonly rendered in your organization and/or in your practice so that you may come to understand your priorities, the concerns and priorities of your colleagues and, through this, those things that really matter where you work.

The exercises developed to facilitate this research may be used by those who, despite being embedded within a particular organization, now find themselves in a situation where they need to come upon their world with 'fresh eyes'. Alternatively, the exercises may be used by consultants who need to form an appreciation of their clients. Equally the exercises may be deployed by those new to a particular organization who need, now, to understand the norms, values and priorities that their colleagues exhibit in and through their storytelling.

You may choose to use the tales you developed in Chapter 3 as the 'data' for this research. Alternatively you may choose to invite your colleagues to share with you the tales that they use to account for their worlds and their concerns. Whether you choose (a) to analyse the tales you have developed or (b) to consider tales harvested from the experience of your colleagues matters little at this stage: The choice is yours.

I do suggest, however, that it will be helpful to locate the tales you select/develop as your research base within, not just one, but a number of the exercises developed below. This co-location will, I suggest, prevent you from developing a top-down account of storytelling. Top-down stories give voice to elite priorities and while these are valid they do tend to strip out the complexity and the polyphony that, as we have learned, enable stories to grasp the essential vitality of our organized existence.

And finally, please don't feel that you need to attempt the exercises as I have arranged these ... you don't.

Exercise one

This exercise invites you to locate the tales, either crafted by you or drawn from the storyworlds of others, according to the broad story-types identified in earlier sections. This exercise, therefore, invites you to reflect upon the extent to which the tales under consideration are:

- epic
- comic
- romantic
- tragic
- tragi-comic
- 'unclassified'.

Epic tales of the organization tend to dominate the narratives developed within 'popular management' texts. This is understandable. These texts are exhortative. They are designed to explain to aspirant managers and, to a lesser extent, recalcitrant employees that change is necessary and, indeed, unavoidable. Furthermore these 'epic' tales generally suggest that those who would lead organizations through programmes of change are worthy of our devotion and truly deserve the colossal material rewards that now accrue, for example, to chief executives. If epic tales dominate your research base this may be a sign that your understanding of the organization has been framed too narrowly.

Epic narratives favour movement and resolution. They are often top-down in orientation and are, consequently, disinclined to reflect the voices and priorities of those located elsewhere within the organization.

Comic tales tend to circulate more widely within organizations, partly because they document the painful absurdities that our organized lives, so often, throw up. If you are hearing comic tales, this may be taken as an indication that you are, at least, tapping some of the counter-narratives that arise in the face of epic tales of endeavour. But caution must be exercised: Your 'comic' tales may be just another form of elite narrative if they laugh 'down' or laugh 'at' 'others' within the organization. So as you analyse the comic tales in your catalogue ask: who and what is the joke?

And what is the basis of the humour? Is it self-deprecating? Or is it a barb designed to snare and, in so doing, to diminish others?

Romantic tales are, as we mentioned before, pretty rare creatures within the organizational world. If the catalogue of tales that you harvested from your colleagues contains accounts that address affairs of the heart, you may take this as a sign that you enjoy a rapport with at least some of your colleagues. If these tales are absent from your catalogue you are plainly missing something.

What will you do to tap into this dimension of your organized experience?

Tragic tales deal with loss. The loss may amount to a minor setback or it may amount to a life-changing or career-ending event. I suggest that when you document your tragic tales you pay special attention to the nature of the loss and the identity of those who have suffered this. Is there a systematic pattern?

Exercise one continued

Do certain people or indeed classes of people routinely lose out? And, if this is the case, does the pattern suggest, for example, that the organization supports or abandons its employees?

Tragi-comic tales are those tales that, for example, leaven loss with comic moments or with comic characters. If you are hearing tales that are tragic-comic in nature it may suggest that you are usefully tapping into the (complex) experiences of your colleagues. Your challenge when encountering tales of this form is, I suggest, to understand the resolution of the tale. To what extent, for example, does the comic moment compensate or account for the loss endured. Did the 'victim' bring the loss upon themselves? And if so might the organization have intervened to prevent or to offset this loss?

Finally, you should at least acknowledge that some of the tales you encounter may resist classification. This resistance to classification may reflect, of course, the essential polyphony of the organized world but if you find yourself in a situation where you simply cannot decide if the tale is, say, comic or tragic, this may indicate that the tale has 'failed' and needs further development in order to deliver a clear and satisfactory resolution for its intended audience.

Exercise two

This exercise is designed to encourage you to reflect upon the extent to which your catalogue of stories narrates (and understands) the organization from the 'top down' or from the 'bottom up'.

Top-down tales of social organization are, of course, rendered by organizational elites. These elites confront particular problems and face pressures and accountabilities not generally shared by those who inhabit the lower reaches of the organization. These top-down tales – often epic in character – tend to focus upon competition, change and customers in an abstracted sense. Top-down tales, therefore, tend to reflect an understanding that managers know best, see further and remain worthy of the support of their subordinates even as they make detrimental changes to staff terms and conditions.

Bottom-up tales of the organization, I suggest, tend not to endorse the altruism voiced in the top-down narratives. Bottom-up tales seek, instead, a more critical engagement with the characters, plotting devices and the motivations projected from the top down.

Bottom-up narratives may be comic. They may, for example, seek to lampoon key decision-makers and the policies they advance. Alternatively they may articulate resignation and/or simple despair for the future.

Your challenge in this exercise (perhaps building upon the initial research undertaken in exercise one) is to understand the perspectives and interests that your catalogue reveals. Is your catalogue narrowly top-down in orientation? If so, your storyworld may be preventing an understanding of 'culture'!

If your catalogue reveals both 'top-down' tales and 'bottom-up' stories your challenge is, I suggest, to understand the perspectives voiced in each. Are the concerns voiced at all congruent? Is there, indeed, any common ground?

If the strategic apex of the organization is being lampooned … does it (do you) deserve to be mocked?

If the voices of the 'bottom up' are resigned or detached … what are you going to do about that?

You may, of course, feel that you now want to develop tales designed to correct a misapprehension. If so, good for you. In fact, I wish you luck.

But please remember that a fundamental disconnect between storyworlds and perspectives may actually signal a need for new policies and new processes that stories will later document and account for!

Exercise three

This exercise is designed to allow you to document what I will term patterns of absence/presence in your storyworld.

Before you undertake this exercise you may wish to undertake just a little more research on your organization so that you might form an understanding of the extent to which your catalogue of stories usefully reflects the character of your workplace.

You may have this information readily to hand. If not ... please spend a few moments gathering some demographic information on your organization or division.

On the page opposite you may wish to jot down a few facts and figures about your workplace so that you have these to hand. You may, for example wish to document:

- overall headcount
- sex/gender split
- average age
- median age
- average/median length of service
- turnover rate
- absence rate
- ethnicity profile
- customer profile
- stakeholder profile
- proportion of women in senior roles
- proportion of BAME persons in senior roles
- anything else that you deem relevant to your working life.

Stories reflect and project priorities; that is why they are central to the narratives developed by 'popular management'. Yet if your tales act, systematically, to exclude components of your workforce or customer base your storyworld will be hollow.

Ask yourself:

Do the characters present in my catalogue usefully reflect the demographics of my workforce?

Do the tales I have developed/harvested/shared meaningfully account for my personal priorities?

Are the heroes of my storyworld (exclusively/predominantly) male and senior?

Is 'commitment' something that employees with dependent children and/or elderly parents can demonstrate within my storyworld?

Do my tales demand total commitment?

What tales are told of those who have quit?

If there is a gap between the reality of your organization and the image projected in and through your storytelling practices what will you do now to remedy this?

Exercise three continued

What steps will you take to ensure that your new storyworld is not, simply, a (nother) top-down projection?

And as you take steps to develop this new storyworld will you, openly and publicly, acknowledge this endeavour as a project that shows your own personal learning?

Exercise four

This exercise has a clear overlap with exercise three. Yet where exercise three sought to reveal patterns of presence and absence in your storyworld this exercise encourages you to reflect upon the manner in which actors in your tales are represented.

Many, if not most, dramas develop a dynamic between dualities; good and evil; change and stability; home and abroad ...

For this exercise, I'd like you to review your storyworld to consider its 'heroes' and its 'villains'.

Is there an 'in' group and an 'out' group within your storyworld? If so on what basis are these roles/ positions allocated?
And is this characterisation fair and consistent?
Could you hope to account for this pattern publicly? And if not ... why not?
If there is a union present within your organizational storyworld how have you chosen to represent this body?
Are processes of 'othering' evident within your storyworld? Are there for example people or functions within your organization that your tales treat disdainfully? If so ... why? Is this outcome sensible and publicly sustainable?

Exercise five

This exercise, again, has some overlap with exercises four and three. I make no apology for this: The organizational world is a complex and ambiguous place. You will need to develop a multi-perspective account of your organization if you are to come to terms with *what* people say, *how* they think and *why* they act in particular ways.

In exercise four you were asked to reflect upon the manner in which your colleagues, customers and stakeholders are represented in your storyworld. In this exercise I will invite you to extend this analysis as you consider who is 'active' and who is more 'passive' within your storytelling.

You may, for example, have female and BAME colleagues present within your dramas of the workplace. But are these people really present? Do they, for example, speak?

Are these people, for example, truly volitional? Or do others speak for them and do things for/to them?

Are your colleagues, customers and/or competitors fully present in your storyworld?

Do your junior colleagues, for example, enjoy full organizational membership in your tales? Or does some combination of age, ethnicity and or sex/gender somehow prevent certain groups from being treated as valued insiders?

And ... if an honest analysis of your storytelling practices does indeed reveal unwarranted patterns of activity/ passivity what will you do now to remedy this? What policies will you now develop and enact to bring authenticity to your storyworld?

And who, now, will act as the hosts of your (new) tales?

Exercise six

This exercise invites you to locate your storytelling catalogue within the analysis developed by Martin et al. (1983). You will recall that in Chapter 1 we drew attention to the 'uniqueness paradox' in organizational storytelling and to the seven basic tales of our organized existence which arise and persist as we attempt to come to terms with the anxieties that arise as a consequence of working with and for others. These story-types, as you may recall, are often couched as a series of questions:

1   Do senior organizational members abide by the rules that they have set down?
2   Is the big boss human?
3   Is the organization meritocratic?
4   Will I get fired?
5   Will the organization assist me to relocate?
6   How does the organization deal with mistakes?
7   How does the organization deal with obstacles?

These seven story forms, while not exhaustive of narrative possibilities, are, Martin et al. (1983) suggest, widespread and enduring. Probing the motivations that underpin these tales, Martin and her colleagues suggest that these questions are related to widespread and persistent concerns which organizational members have with respect to:

• equality
• security
• control.

Stories developed in response to questions one, two and three (above) deal with concerns related to equality and inequality at work. Stories developed in response to questions four, five and six, in contrast, relate to tensions formed around a security–insecurity duality. Stories developed in response to question seven reflect concerns with respect to control and autonomy in this context.

Your task in this exercise is two-fold.

First, does your storyworld reflect, fully, these questions?

Does your catalogue, for example, actually reflect each of the questions presented above? And if not, which questions are absent from your catalogue?

If your catalogue is incomplete what does this say of you and your storyworld? And what, if anything will you do to develop or, perhaps more pertinently, to uncover these missing elements from the bottom up?

Your second task is to consider the manner in which your storyworld responds to the questions detailed above.

Does your catalogue, for example, affirm that 'the big boss' is indeed human? Or does it represent him/ her in a different and altogether less wholesome fashion?

Exercise six continued

Do your tales of organization affirm that the senior members of your organization are consistent in their conduct? And if not why have these narrative arisen? And are such tales widespread in your organization and persistently shared?

And finally … what steps might you take now to redeem this position?

If your storyworld suggests that senior members of the collective are inconsistent and/or uncaring will you change your conduct? And if so … what will you do to signal your personal commitment to this change?

Exercise seven

Last, but not least, this exercise invites you to submit your storyworld to the Bechdel–Wallace test.

The Bechdel–Wallace test offers a measure of the representation of women in fiction and although it now exists in a number of variants asks three, core questions:

1 Does the work feature at least two women who talk to each other?
2 In conversation do these women talk about something other than a man?
3 Does the work identify these women by name?

I do accept that – depending upon the narrative form – you may for very good reason choose to anonymize your tales. I will therefore accept that some of your tales, which usefully represent your female colleagues will pass on just two of the three components listed above. Nonetheless the test remains:

How many of your tales identify two female colleagues and place these individuals within a setting where they speak to each other and make choices for themselves?

Equally we might ask: How many of your tales feature a female employee and, say, a female customer talking as adults and making serious decisions?

If your storytelling fails or is deficient according to the Bechdel–Wallace test what will you do now to reconfigure your storytelling?

Will your new tales be accepted as authentic? And … if not why not?

And finally, who will host your reconfigured tales?

Concluding comments

This, the final chapter of our workbook, has been developed to allow you:

a   to research your organization's storyworld;
b   to reflect upon your own storytelling practices;
c   to allow you to sketch an agenda for change that recognizes:

   i   the tensions between sensegiving and sensemaking narratives; and
   ii   the persistent anxieties that shape our experience of working and our perspectives on our colleagues.

This workbook has been propelled by a central belief which, as we conclude, is worthy of restatement in terms of modality (see Latour, 1987):

1   Storytelling is a vital constituent of social organization.
2   Sustained and critical reflection on organizational storytelling can provide useful insight on organizational dynamics and priorities ... in short: culture.
3   The careful reanalysis of organizational storytelling offers each of us the tools necessary to reveal, to recover and to redeem voices and perspectives, too often, written out by the narratives of 'popular management'.
4   Honest reflection on your organizational storytelling practices will provide the insights and the data necessary to allow you to develop the projections necessary to intervene purposefully in the norms, values and beliefs that constitute the cultural formation that is your organization.
5   Success in storytelling cannot be guaranteed.
6   Failure awaits those who cannot appreciate the manner in which audiences may (a) reject tales and (b) punish storytellers who come off as arrogant and inauthentic.

You may now have questions. Indeed you may have insights and observations that will allow me to improve and to refine future editions of this workbook should these be called for ...

I don't pretend to have all the answers ... so I'd love to hear from you about your experiences.

You can find me at david@gaininsight.org.uk.

References

Latour, B. (1987) *Science in Action*, Harvard University Press: Cambridge, MA.
Martin, J., Feldman, M.S., Hatch, M.J. and Sitkin, S.B. (1983) 'The Uniqueness Paradox in Organizational Storytelling', *Administrative Science Quarterly*, 28: 438–453.